How We Choose A President

HOW WE CHOOSE
A PRESIDENT

THE ELECTION YEAR

Revised Edition

by LEE LEARNER GRAY

illustrated by Stanley Stamaty

ST. MARTIN'S PRESS, New York

for Ned, Harold, and Josh

ACKNOWLEDGMENTS

This new edition has been revised in collaboration with Lawrence E. Gray, my husband. To him go my thanks for his advice and help as a skillful co-author, a perceptive critic, and a stern editor during many fruitful months of working together.

Thanks are due, too, to Richard M. Scammon, director of the Elections Research Center, Washington, D.C., and to Alice McGillivray, also of the Center, for sharing their expertise on voting problems.

My thanks, also, as in the original edition:

—to my parents, for their constant encouragement and faith;

—and, for their valuable suggestions, to Irma Simonton Black, chairman of the Publications Department at Bank Street College of Education in New York City; and Esther Rotkin, chairman of the Social Studies Department of Takoma Park Junior High School, Montgomery County, Maryland.

CONTENTS

How We Choose A President

1

A Glance at the Year

A presidential election is coming.

It is late summertime in the United States, and Americans are turning their attention to the important job of electing a President. Soon the entire country will be caught up in a coast-to-coast election campaign.

Election Day is months away . . . September . . . October . . . November. The first Tuesday after the first Monday in November is Election Day, when the voters will choose the man who will be President of the United States for the next four years.

But already the hot August air is heavy with talk about that far off November day, and about the two men who are running for the Presidency. These men were chosen just a few weeks ago. The news flashed out across the cities, the mountains, the plains:

Note: Words set in boldface type are defined in the Glossary on page 139.

BOYLE NOMINATED BY DEMOCRATIC PARTY! . . . WEBBER NAMED REPUBLICAN CANDIDATE!

Now the country knows that these men have been **nominated** as the two major **candidates** in the presidential election campaign. Millions of Americans are listening to Webber and Boyle, arguing and reading about Webber and Boyle.

A businessman in Massachusetts, hurrying to work, glances at fat, black newspaper headlines: BOYLE BLASTS WEBBER ON INCOME TAX PLAN . . . WEBBER ATTACKS BOYLE FOREIGN AID POLICY

Steelworkers stand at a factory gate in Pennsylvania and argue about whether Webber should be President.

A sunburned woman lying on a California beach turns on her radio to hear Boyle tell about his tax policy.

A farmer in Iowa settles down in front of his television set to hear a Democrat and a Republican argue about whose candidate will win the race for the Presidency.

Who are Boyle and Webber, and how did they become presidential candidates? What is the Democratic party, the Republican party? What do the parties have to do with the nominations, the candidates, the election? What goes on during a presidential election campaign?

The most active part of the race between the two candidates is usually crowded into nine or ten hurried weeks from Labor Day, early in September, to Election Day, early in November. But the election campaign actually begins many months before September, and its grand finale does not come until several months after Election Day. A presidential election year stretches from one January to the next.

What Happens During an Election Year

Election-year activities follow a script, just as a movie or a play does. No matter who the actors are, the script will run according to a schedule, with each act taking place during a certain time.

Act I   (*January-June*) The Search for
                Candidates
Act II   (*July-August*) The Nomination of
                Candidates
Act III (*September-November*) The Campaign
Act IV (*November*) Election Day
Epilogue (*January*) The New President Takes
                Over

There you have a political script. The story of how we elect our President is a story of **politics** in the United States, for our presidential election is run by **political parties.**

In our country today we have two major political parties: the Republican party and the Democratic party. Our presidential campaign is usually a race between the candidates of these two major parties. During our history we have had minority parties also; and we still do. These **third parties** add lively footnotes to the story of American politics. By introducing ideas different from those of the major parties they have had a real influence on the country. But they do not win presidential elections.

Our story of the presidential election year will concentrate on the two major parties and the parts they play in searching for candidates, nominating their candidates, running their campaigns, and winning or losing on Election Day.

Election Sights and Sounds

Once every four years during your life as an American citizen, you will live through a presidential election. What will you see and hear during that campaign year?

Act I . . . The Search for Candidates

You will see both political parties examining their leaders. Each party is trying to find its most promising presidential candidate, for each wants to nominate the man with the best chance of winning the election.

You will see leading Republicans and Democrats work to capture their party's nomination. You will hear Democrats argue with Democrats, Republicans argue with Republicans, for within each party there are many opposing groups. The groups often have different views and favor different men, but within each party all the groups must somehow agree on one man to be their party's candidate.

Act II . . . The Nomination of Candidates

You will see each party nominate its man at a national convention. You will watch on television as Democrats, or Republicans gather in a huge, hot auditorium. You will hear speeches and cheers and brass bands; and you will see delegates waving flags and parading up and down the aisles of the auditorium. Out of these noisy scenes will come each party's presidential candidate.

Act III . . . The Campaign

For several months the candidates will make speeches in every corner of the country. Each party will work long and hard to convince people to vote for its candidate. Many millions of citizens will be reading, thinking, arguing about which candidate would be the better President.

Neighbors will ring your doorbell to give you campaign leaflets saying, "Vote for Webber!" or "Vote for Boyle!" You will see newspaper pages covered with campaign news about Boyle and Webber. On radio and television you will hear people asking questions, giving answers, making speeches, urging, "Vote for . . . vote for . . . vote for . . . !"

Act IV . . . Election Day

Suddenly the country will be quiet. On a Tuesday morning in early November, voters will stand patiently in line. You will see them in your town, waiting to enter voting booths where they will pull levers on voting machines or mark X's on ballots to show which man they want for President.

On Election Night you will listen to the radio or watch the television screen as the election returns come in. You will study scoreboards listing voting figures from every state in the nation. At last the figures will show which man the voters have chosen to lead our nation for the next four years.

Epilogue . . . The New President Takes Over

January's grand finale takes place in Washington, the nation's capital, where the President will be **inau-**

gurated. As the campaign year ends, a new presidential administration begins.

These are the sights you will see, the sounds you will hear, during a presidential election year.

Seeing and hearing, however, are not enough to help you understand exactly what is going on. The sights and sounds take on meaning only if you know the reasons for what happens. In this book we shall look behind the scenes to learn why these things happen as they do. We shall glance occasionally at our history, too, for history sets the stage for today's action.

What Does It All Mean?

First, it is important to understand why there is so much coast-to-coast excitement connected with a presidential campaign:

The Presidency is our government's only national elective office.*

The **Governor** of your state is elected by the people of your state only. So are the men and women who represent you in your state **legislature** and who make laws for your state.

Senators and **Representatives** in **Congress** pass laws for the entire country. But each Senator represents

---

* The Vice-Presidency is a national elective position too, but the Vice President is not elected separately. His name appears on the ballot as the presidential candidate's running mate. Citizens vote for him as part of the party's national ticket.

just one state; he's elected only by the people in his state. A Representative is elected only by the people in one district of his state: they are the only people he must represent.

The President alone is selected by the votes of all Americans. He is the only elected official who represents all of us; and that makes our presidential elections different from our other elections.

Our presidential elections capture the spirit of the whole nation. Observing this coast-to-coast interest, a visitor from another country once wrote this description of American presidential elections:

> Speaking and writing and canvassing are common to elections all over the world. What is peculiar to America is the amazing development of the "demonstration" as a means for raising enthusiasm. For three months, processions, usually with brass bands, flags, badges, crowds of cheering spectators, are the order of the day and night from end to end of the country. . . . The parade and procession business, the crowds, the torches, the badges, the flags, the shouting, all this . . . keeps up the "boom," and an American election is held to be, truly or falsely, largely a matter of booming.*

But then this visitor went on to explain the seriousness and significance behind the "booming":

* This description was written by an Englishman, James Bryce, in his book *The American Commonwealth*. Bryce wrote this long ago, in 1895, and our presidential elections are still booming. We may have given up the torchlight parades, but we have substituted jet planes, motorcades, and television debates.

> . . . it is the choice of one officer by the whole country, a supreme political act in which every voter has a share, and the same share. . . .

It's an odd combination: the booming ballyhoo that we show on the outside, and the quiet seriousness that we feel inside. Our American poet Walt Whitman put it this way:

> I know nothing grander, better exercise, better digestion, more positive proof of the past, the triumphant result of faith in human kind, than a well-contested American national election.

Probably all Americans feel this without ever thinking it out and putting it into words. In a way, our rousing election campaign is a gigantic, coast-to-coast party that celebrates something very precious to us: our great opportunity to choose the man who will head our government.

Nowhere else in the world do so many people freely cast their votes to choose the man who will lead them. Because the Presidency is a position of power, choosing the President gives *us* great power in molding our country.

The President's Power—and Ours

As the head of our government, the President of the United States has broad powers. These powers are set forth in the basic law of our country, the Constitution, which was written in 1787 by the men who founded our nation.

The Constitution says, in part, that the President's duties shall be:

> to be commander in chief of the armed forces;
>
> to enforce the Constitution and the laws made by Congress;
>
> to make treaties with other nations (with the Senate's consent);
>
> to appoint (with the Senate's consent) Supreme Court justices, ambassadors to other countries, department heads, and other high officials;
>
> to keep Congress informed on the state of the Union, and to recommend necessary bills to Congress;
>
> to sign into law or veto bills passed by Congress; and
>
> to call special sessions of Congress in times of emergency.

What a tremendous job for just one man! We expect the President to protect us and to guard our rights. We expect him to handle our dealings with other countries and to choose many men who will help run our government. We expect him to have the wisdom to know what laws will be best for the nation.

No wonder we think and talk and argue for months before we finally choose the man to fill this job. We know that the President holds vast power, and it is our privilege to give this power to just one man, every four years.

Of course, the head of any government must have power in order to lead the country. But in different countries, power comes to the leaders in different ways.

In some countries, power is passed down from father to son, a man becoming king because his father was king. In other countries we have seen men seize physical control of the government. There, men use guns, war planes, and marching men to grasp and maintain power. In many countries, the man in the top position is selected by a small group of the country's leaders. There, the power to choose a leader does not lie directly with the people; instead, that power belongs to the people's representatives, the men they elect to run their government.

But in the United States, the power to choose is in the hands of the people. A man becomes President because he is chosen by the voters in a national election.

Though today's world has many other democracies, there is none where so many people share the power to vote freely for their national leader. And there is none where this power has been the law of the land for so very many years.

In other, older countries, the people had to chip away at the absolute power of the king to gain a voice in their government. But the United States was *founded* as a republic—a nation in which the power to govern comes from the people, rather than from a king. When the writers of our Constitution proclaimed that "we the people" were establishing the United States, they set up a republican form of government; and they took a step toward democracy that no other country had ever taken.

Ours was the first country to have a written constitution asserting that power comes from and belongs to the people, and providing for the election of representatives—including a President—who would use the power for the people. American citizens have given this power to a President every four years since 1789, when white-wigged George Washington was elected our first President.

As we shall see later, Washington and the other early Presidents were not nominated and elected as today's Presidents are. Changes have been made because the democracy of 1789 was not the same democracy we know today. The power of *all* the people to elect their President was not stated in the Constitution; that privilege came later.

What the Constitution Says—and Doesn't Say

When the men who founded our country gathered in Philadelphia in the hot summer of 1787 to write a constitution, they well knew that they were creating a new kind of government. They wanted to guarantee the liberty and independence of their struggling young country. They were dedicated to the idea that free men could rule themselves without a king.

The leaders at that Constitutional Convention were wise men who understood much about government and about the power needed to run a government. The founding fathers were wary of giving too much power to any one branch of the government. Cleverly and carefully, they divided the new government's powers.

The Constitution says that the Congress shall have power to make the laws. It says that the President shall have power to enforce the laws. It says that the Supreme Court shall have power to decide whether the laws are in agreement with the Constitution. And, in order to protect everyone's rights, it guarantees that certain other powers shall be reserved for the states or for the people.

But the great power to elect the President was not given to all the people. The Constitution said that the President should be elected by electors—a small group of special people appointed by the states. Special people, mind you; not ordinary citizens, not all the citizens. This great power to choose everyone's President was reserved for a few special citizens.

The democratic ideas of 1787 simply did not include the concept that the common people had the right to make such an important decision as choosing a President. The authors of the Constitution *did* want a government that would protect everyone's rights, a government in which everyone would be fairly represented. They *did* believe in government for the people, in government of the people. But government *by* the people—with all the citizens having the power to vote for the country's leader—that was a democratic idea that developed later.

If this seems strange to you, you must realize that the very thought of having a republican form of government with an elected leader was a revolutionary idea in the eighteenth century. Then most countries were monarchies; their leaders were kings who were born to leadership, who inherited their power, and who ruled for life. So it was considered quite a triumph when the Constitution provided for the election, every four years, of a President whose specific powers derived from the people.

The Constitution not only omits giving all the people the power to elect the President. It tells us nothing about how presidential candidates shall be nominated.* It does not say a word about political parties, national conventions, or election campaigns. Nowhere does this basic law of the land spell out the exciting part that today's citizens and parties play in choosing a President.

Would the writers of the Constitution be astonished

---

* Though it does not mention nominations, the Constitution does specify a few basic requirements for a presidential candidate: he must be a natural-born citizen, thirty-five years old, and a resident of the United States for fourteen years.

to see what has happened to American presidential elections? Would they be dismayed by the idea of our two major political parties? By our noisy nominating conventions? By our booming campaigns that send candidates hurrying to television studios, to small-town airports, to big-city auditoriums? By the long lines of citizens waiting to vote on that Tuesday in November?

The founding fathers did not plan things this way, but they might not be surprised after all. They wisely wrote a Constitution that has been flexible enough to allow for many changes. It allowed for the growth of political parties, which did not exist in 1787. And along with the growth of parties came the great change giving citizens the power to choose their leader. How and why these changes occurred we shall see as we trace the steps involved in nominating and electing a President today.

2

Act One . . .
The Search for Candidates

It is the beginning of January, the start of a new year. This is a year with a date divisible by four, a year when millions of Americans will elect a President.*

On this January morning, very few of those millions are thinking of next November. In some parts of the United States, boys and girls toss snowballs as they walk to school; men dig their cars out of snowbanks. Elsewhere, boys and girls squint against the bright warm sun, and women dig in their flower gardens. Everywhere, people talk about the weather, about their jobs, about how they celebrated New Year's Eve.

* The 1968 population of the United States includes over 116 million citizens of voting age. (18 years old in Georgia and Kentucky; 19 in Alaska; 20 in Hawaii; and 21 in all other states.)

Between 74 and 75 million of these 116 million are expected to vote in the 1968 presidential election. Some reasons why the remaining 40 million will not vote are discussed on page 107.

Next November is far from their minds; it's ten long months in the future.

But in every one of our fifty states, you can find small groups of men and women who have long been planning for the presidential election. For many months, even several years, they have been holding meetings and conferences. They have been studying election figures from the last presidential campaign. They have been examining maps of their states and lists of voters within their states.

With all this talking, studying, examining, they are trying to answer one question: Who should be our candidate in next November's election?

The people trying to answer this question are active members of our two major political parties; they're Democrats and Republicans. They are, in a word, **politicians.**

What Is a Politician?

Most Americans consider themselves either Democrats or Republicans. The experts estimate that few citizens—roughly only about 20 per cent—are **independent voters.**

However, the majority of Democrats and Republicans have little to do with their parties except to vote for them on Election Day. They may be enrolled **party members;** but not many are active enough to be called politicians.

What makes a politician different from a citizen who simply thinks of himself as a Democrat or a Republican?

Some Republican and Democratic politicians are professionals; they're full-time politicians. Politics is their business. Day after day, year in and year out, they work at running their parties and at trying to win elections. A professional politician may be an elected official who helps to make our laws or run our government. Or he may be a party official who directs campaigns to elect his party's candidates.

Others are amateur politicians. They may be lawyers, businessmen, housewives, mechanics, shopkeepers, farmers, writers. Whatever their jobs, they give much spare time to working for their parties. They are citizens who try to influence their government by being politically active.

Without all of these politicians, we could not carry on a national election campaign. It is the parties' job to select the presidential candidates. Each party will face that job next summer at its nominating convention. From January until July, Republicans and Democrats will be preparing for the conventions and searching for possible candidates.

A party's search for a presidential candidate is an exhausting job. Actually, it is fifty different searches, for this national manhunt is carried on separately in each of our fifty states. In every state, party members must choose the delegates who will represent them at the nominating convention. At the same time, each state's party members will be trying to decide which man their delegates should support at the convention.

These choices require special elections, state conventions, endless conferences, speeches, campaigns. In January, each party's politicians know that they face six months of hard work before they can finally nominate a presidential candidate.

Why does the search for candidates center in the states? You can answer that question when you understand how our parties are organized.

How Parties are Organized

Each political party is organized into national, state, and local units, just as our government is.

The smallest local unit is the **precinct** club; this is the **grassroots** level of the party. Here you will find the party's amateur politicians, the people who go out and ring neighbors' doorbells during an election campaign. The precinct committee is the party's closest link with the voters.

Each precinct is represented on the county committee, the next local party unit. The county chairman's political job is to know the voters in his precincts and to elect his party's candidates for local offices. Whether he's an amateur or a professional, he keeps in close touch with the party leaders in his state.

Politicians working on the state level are more likely to be professionals. The party's State Central Committee must raise campaign funds, direct statewide election campaigns, help build up local groups throughout the state. Running a state organization is a full-time job; it's handled by the chairman of the State Central Committee.

The **National Committee** ties together the entire party organization; its members come from the state parties. This committee meets actively only once every four years when it helps to direct the presidential campaign.

As you can see, the fifty state organizations carry the big load of running the party, year in and year out. Each state party is a separate, independent unit.

There is a practical reason for this: the Constitution says that the state governments shall run all elections. Each state makes its own election laws; the laws of the fifty states are all quite different. And Democrats and Republicans in each state must organize and operate according to the laws of their own state.

There are two other reasons for the importance of the party's state organization. State delegations play a big role at the national nominating convention. And later, in November, the states are all-important when the votes for President are counted.

For all these reasons, the men and women who run each state organization are often the most powerful

politicians in the party. These people have moved up
to state leadership after being active on precinct and
county committees; they know voters throughout their
state. They know what kind of candidate will be popular with these voters. Often they have the most to say
about which men will be considered as presidential
candidates.

Where Do Candidates Come From?

Right now, in January, politicians in fifty states are
asking one another, "Who can win for us?"

This question has been on their minds for a long,
long time, for party leaders are constantly looking
ahead to the next election. In fact, there's an old political saying that a new campaign begins the morning
after Election Day.

The leaders of each party hope to find a man who
will be wise and strong enough to lead the country
well. But above all, each party wants a candidate who
can win the Presidency.

In searching for this man, politicians are most likely
to consider Governors, Senators, **Cabinet** members,
and perhaps **Congressmen.*** Why is there such a small
group of possible candidates?

---

* Congressmen are seldom as well-known as Senators since there
are 435 Congressmen as opposed to only 100 Senators. But an outstanding Congressman who has served for many years may sometimes
be considered. Cabinet members are the only men in this group who
are appointed, not elected, to office. However, as the President's
advisers, Cabinet members are government "insiders." What's more,
they are often men who have had much political experience.

A presidential candidate usually must be a man who is well-known to voters throughout the country, a man with an impressive record of public service, and a man who understands how the government operates. These "musts" tend to limit the choice to men who have had experience with the national government, or in running a state government.

The politicians also want a man who has a strong, attractive personality, and whose opinions will appeal to independent voters as well as to party members. They hope he will come from a large state, and that he will be an expert at campaigning and winning elections. A man who has recently won an election, in his own state, for Senator or Governor has added much to his appeal as a possible presidential candidate; one who has just lost such an election has almost surely killed his chances of being considered.

Occasionally, politicians find that their most attractive presidential candidate is a man without experience in government. In 1940, the Republicans nominated a businessman, Wendell Willkie, who lost the election. Again, in 1952, the Republicans chose an army general, Dwight D. Eisenhower, who did win the Presidency. But presidential candidates without government experience are exceptions. Since 1900, all of our Presidents except Eisenhower have been former Governors, Senators, or Cabinet members.

These, then, are the men who are studied from state

to state, from coast to coast, by Democratic and Republican politicians. Often the politicians within a state cannot agree on a choice; they split into groups favoring different men. Each group campaigns hard, before the convention, to win support for its man.

The Candidates Make News

Each man, in turn, is busily tending to his own campaigning. Some of this campaigning is done quietly; some is carried on with much publicity. During the past year, each would-be candidate* has visited many states to talk privately with leading politicians and perhaps with some grassroots party workers too. He has also made speeches, held press conferences, appeared on television programs, written magazine articles. Every presidential hopeful has two goals: to build his support among the party's politicians; and to keep his name before the country's voters.

Each of these Governors, Senators, Cabinet members hopes to be nominated for the Presidency. Some, perhaps, have been dreaming of the White House for

---

* Unfortunately, no one has invented a single, convenient word to describe these men who are considered as possible candidates. You will hear them called would-be candidates, presidential hopefuls, nomination-seekers, possible nominees, presidential timber. For convenience, they're sometimes called simply "candidates." But you must remember that, before the conventions, all of these men are *candidates for the parties' nominations*. At each convention, one will be nominated as a *candidate for the Presidency*.

years. But as the presidential election year begins, no man may yet be willing to **toss his hat into the ring.** Each is still playing a waiting game, waiting to see where he stands with his party's politicians and with the voters.

The voters may still be shoveling snow and digging in flower gardens. But soon many will be talking politics, for during January and February the campaigning of politicians and candidates makes front-page news.

In Columbus, Ohio, Senator Webber steps off a plane from Washington, D.C. He is greeted by the chairman of Ohio's Republican State Committee. Senator Webber is a Utah Republican. This is news. Reporters interview the Senator and the state chairman. Are they going to talk presidential politics? Is the Senator about to toss his hat in the ring? The Senator shakes his head. "No comment," he says. But news of the meeting goes out across the wires to the rest of the country. From Maine to Hawaii, newspaper readers keep their eyes on Senator Webber.

In San Francisco, California, Governor Boyle—a Democrat—is making a speech to a conference of businessmen. He discusses business conditions in his own state; then he talks about laws that Congress should pass to help businessmen. Why is the Governor commenting on national affairs? His listeners wonder whether he plans to seek the Democratic presidential nomination. A television newscaster in the audience makes a note of this, and once again the word goes out across the nation. From Alaska to Florida, people start watching Governor Boyle.

In Gary, Indiana, a housewife answers her doorbell; she finds herself face-to-face with a political question. The man standing in her doorway is a **poll-taker** who is working on a **public-opinion survey.** He asks her this question: "Here is a list of men who have been mentioned as possible presidential candidates for the Republican party. Which man would you like to see nominated?"

The housewife's answer will be added to those of several thousand other citizens questioned throughout the country. The results of this **poll,** and of many others about the coming election, will appear in big-city papers and in small-town papers. They will be read by Senator Webber and by Governor Boyle . . . by the Republican party chairman in Ohio and by the businessmen in California . . . by the Indiana house-wife and by millions of other Americans who are growing more and more interested in the coming presidential election.

The Primary Elections

Before January ends, a certain political event in New Hampshire makes front-page headlines:

BOYLE AND OGILVY ENTER
DEMOCRATIC PRIMARY
IN NEW HAMPSHIRE

Now the country knows that these two men have tossed their hats into the presidential ring.

Governor Boyle and Senator Ogilvy are both Democrats. They will be running against each other in the Democratic primary in New Hampshire, for a primary election is an election within one party. New Hampshire's primary, early in March, is the first of many such state elections.*

A **presidential primary election** is more like a popularity contest than an actual election. On Primary Day in New Hampshire, **registered** Democrats who go to the **polls** will be given Democratic **ballots** bearing the names of Boyle and Ogilvy. By marking an X beside one name or the other, each Democrat will show which man he prefers as his party's candidate.

This vote will not make either man the party's presidential candidate. It will simply show which man

---

* Fifteen states hold presidential primaries: New Hampshire, Wisconsin, Illinois, New Jersey, Massachusetts, Pennsylvania, Indiana, Ohio, Nebraska, West Virginia, Maryland, Oregon, Florida, California, and South Dakota. A sixteenth primary is held in the District of Columbia. The state laws regarding primaries vary tremendously. Alabama and Arkansas have laws permitting primaries, but seldom hold them. Texas law does not provide for a presidential primary, and none had been held in that state until 1964 when the Texas Republican party did run a presidential primary. The exact details of New Hampshire's primary are different from those in each other state.

is more popular with Democrats voting in the New Hampshire primary. The winner of this "popularity" election will boost his standing with Democratic politicians and voters throughout the country.

Boyle and Ogilvy have another reason for entering this primary election. New Hampshire's delegates to the Democratic nominating convention will be chosen by the Democrats voting in the state primary. Some of the people who are running for delegates' positions may pledge themselves for either Boyle or Ogilvy. Pledged delegates are bound to support their man at the nominating convention.

Primary Day in New Hampshire will be an election day for the state's Republicans, too. Two Republicans, Senator Webber and Governor Bonifant, have entered the Republican primary. Registered Republicans will mark Republican ballots, choosing between Bonifant and Webber, and also selecting New Hampshire's delegates to the Republican nominating convention.

Throughout February, there will be two election campaigns going on in New Hampshire. Democrats will meet Boyle and Ogilvy, will hear them talk and argue about what is best for the country. Republicans will listen to Webber and Bonifant, will shake hands with them in supermarkets, will ask them questions at streetcorner meetings.

This is the time when each candidate is experimenting with campaign methods and ideas—trying to discover how he can best put himself across with the voters. To find a winning approach, a candidate may consult with a public relations firm or an advertising agency. These are companies whose business ordinarily is to sell a product or an idea to the public. They use magazine and newspaper advertisements, radio and television commercials; and they work to build up favorable publicity for their clients. In recent years, more and more candidates have been turning to these firms for help in creating an "image" that will appeal to voters.

Across the country, politicians and voters will be watching New Hampshire's primary results. Which Republican, which Democrat, has more vote-getting strength? How many convention votes can each man line up?

Strategy in the Primaries

The other states' presidential primaries take place during April, May, and June. Not every candidate will enter every primary; these campaigns require much time, energy, and money. Each man, with his supporters, maps out a different strategy. Each decides to run in the states that can do him the most good.

Governor Boyle chooses the larger states which will have more voting strength at the nominating convention. The Governor hopes that victories in these large states will help to bring him support from other groups of convention delegates.

Senator Ogilvy, a Westerner, picks Eastern states where he seems least likely to win because he is not well-known. If he can win in the East and so prove that he is popular there as well as in the West, he may win the support of politicians who hesitated to back him earlier.

Senator Webber enters the primary in Ohio, his home state. He has no opponents here; his name alone will appear on the Republican ballot. He is hoping to prove that he has a great deal of support. He is bound to win; how well he will win is the important question. His success will be measured by the number of party members who show their enthusiasm for him by taking the trouble to vote in an uncontested election.

Running in presidential primaries is a risky political game. If a man wins the primaries he enters, he stays in the nominations race. If he loses several primaries, or even a single important one, he will probably be forced out of the running.

In addition to the main contenders, other names will come up during the primaries. Often, they are men who are more popular with grassroots party workers than they are with the party leaders.

Sometimes, interested citizens use the primaries to promote the candidacy of a man they admire. This can be done through a write-in campaign. Voters are urged to write this man's name on their ballots to show that they prefer him as a candidate, instead of voting for a man whose name is already printed on the ballot.

Sometimes, a man whose ideas are not widely accepted by party leaders may enter some of his party's primaries to test his strength among the voters. If he shows enough strength in these elections, he may gain more influence within his party and be considered as a possible candidate. However, if party leaders won't accept him in spite of voter support, he may decide to run for the Presidency on a third-party ticket.

As a third-party candidate, he is not likely to have a realistic chance of winning the presidential election. Organizing a new party and getting on the ballot in 50 states is an extremely complicated, difficult task. But he might take millions of votes away from the two major-party candidates, in the states where the third party does get on the ballot. With these votes, he might be in a very powerful position after Election Day. This is possible because of the special way votes are counted in presidential elections.*

How the Primaries Shape Up

During these pre-convention months, the country's political scene comes into better focus:

* See pages 116-118 and page 132 for explanations of how these votes are counted and how a third-party candidate might affect the voting results.

The search for candidates is narrowing down as the losers in the primaries drop out of the race.

Politicians in the states holding primaries are stirring up the interest of less active party members. Politicians favoring each candidate campaign for party votes. They urge registered Democrats and Republicans to go to the polls and choose between Boyle and Ogilvy, between Webber and Bonifant.*

Citizens in every state, watching the candidates in action, are making decisions about these men. The primary campaigns help the voters learn what each man stands for, where and how he would lead the country.

More and more Americans talk about politics and political issues. How can we achieve peace among the nations of the world? What laws should be passed for the good of the country? These are issues being debated by the candidates; thoughtful citizens are beginning to discuss them also.

The Search in Other States

Though presidential primaries make the biggest headlines, only one-third of the states hold these elec-

* Not all Republicans and Democrats vote in the primaries. Many cannot because they have not registered; others are so inactive that they overlook the primaries. Thus they lose the chance to have a part in nominating their party's presidential candidate. Voters who prefer to be independent usually have no opportunity to take part in the nominating process. But interestingly enough, the independent voters often hold the balance of power in the presidential election in November.

tions. Parties in the other states are making pre-convention plans, too.

In each of these non-primary states, politicians are searching and candidates are campaigning. Democratic and Republican parties in every state face political battles as they choose their delegates to the national nominating convention. Most often, these delegates are chosen at a state convention of party members.*

These people are sent to the state convention by the local party units. When they meet, they may not all favor the same presidential hopeful. Each group tries to name delegates who will vote for its candidate at the national convention. Sometimes one group is powerful enough to dominate the state convention. Then the state's delegates may be instructed to support a certain candidate for the nomination.

This kind of pre-convention campaigning doesn't encourage inactive Democrats and Republicans to take part in the search for candidates. In these non-primary states, the party battles seldom stir up much interest among the voters. Here, the professional and amateur politicians choose the delegates who will support Boyle or Ogilvy, Webber or Bonifant.

* The procedure is not always this simple. Choice of national delegates is a complicated tangle: it may involve local meetings, local elections, district conventions, or special state committees, as well as state conventions. Each state party must follow the state's election laws and its own party rules. There are actually one hundred different methods for selecting delegates to the national convention.

Many politicians here work for other candidates, too. These states are good campaign grounds for presidential hopefuls who do not enter primaries.

Since primaries are so risky, some candidates avoid the long, costly election campaigns. Primaries are not the only road to winning the nomination. The nonprimary states offer other chances for a man to win support and line up convention delegates.

Working behind the scenes is Congressman Revere, a Democrat. He has been quietly sounding out his strength among Democratic politicians throughout the North, East, West, and South. His friends in Congress have been urging politicians back home to send delegates favoring Revere to the national convention. Revere has been in Congress for many years, they argue, and he is well-known to voters everywhere. Perhaps there is a good chance that many Democratic delegates will turn to Revere if the primary winners are not strong enough at the convention.

Working to keep his name in the headlines is Secretary of Agriculture Johansen, a member of the President's Cabinet and a Republican. By traveling and making speeches, he has built up grassroots support. Johansen's policies have been popular with the farmers; the Midwest is all for him. His appealing personality has won him many friends elsewhere too. Almost any delegate from a Midwestern state would probably name Johansen as his first choice for the nomination.

And perhaps the solid farm vote at the Republican convention can swing enough delegates over to Johansen.

As the conventions approach, politicians in each party ask these questions about every candidate: Does he have enough delegate support to win the nomination? Could he win the Presidency for our party?

3

A Backward Glance...
at Politicians, Parties,
and the Presidency

As you watch Democrats and Republicans at work before their conventions, you see that nominations and political parties are woven together as closely as two threads in a piece of material. Can you believe that the earliest Americans tried to plan a government that would be entirely free of political parties? At first that was the hope of the leaders who founded the United States.

The founding fathers labored to write a Constitution that would unify the people in the thirteen states. They feared that political parties, with different ideas about running the country, would divide the citizens of the struggling new United States.

Most of all, they wanted a President who would

not take sides with any opposing groups that might develop. They did not want the nation's leader to owe his position to a powerful organization that had campaigned for him.

The founding fathers did not prohibit parties in the Constitution. In fact, most of the country's leaders already belonged to one of two political groups: the Federalists or the Anti-Federalists.* But they all wanted to find a way to prevent parties from becoming powerful national organizations that might influence the Presidency.

This problem, they thought, might be solved by having the states run all elections. They reasoned that if each state handled its own elections, political arguments would be confined within the borders of each state. Political organizations would not spread across state boundaries. It would be impossible for strong national parties to develop.

They quickly discovered that they were wrong. Political arguments divided the national government almost as soon as George Washington was elected President in 1789.

How Parties Developed

Those were dangerous times for the young country. The idea of a republic was new and strange in the

---

* The Federalists wanted a strong national government that would make decisions for all the states. The Anti-Federalists argued that the states should be stronger and should make the important decisions.

world, an experiment. No one was certain how a country should solve its problems without a powerful king to make the decisions. And the United States faced many problems. The government needed money; it could not pay its debts. The states were quarreling with one another about boundaries and trade regulations. The country could not settle its arguments with England and France.

As the problems mounted during Washington's first administration, the men running the government could not agree on solutions. Two members of Washington's Cabinet—Thomas Jefferson and Alexander Hamilton—argued for opposing policies. Although Washington stood apart from their arguments, many of the country's other leaders took sides with these two men.

Hamilton, the leader of the Federalists, proposed plans that would strengthen the Federal government. Hamilton believed that a powerful national government was essential to stabilize the country and to pull the nation out of debt. He argued that a strong central government was needed to make the states work together; it would also win respect abroad for the young country.

Jefferson led the Democratic-Republicans, the group which had developed from the Anti-Federalists; they wanted to strengthen the states' powers. Jefferson insisted that the real power in a democracy belonged to the states and the citizens within the states—

the farmers and planters, the hunters and trappers on the frontiers, the artisans and craftsmen in the cities. Jefferson felt that Hamilton's policies favored bankers, merchants, manufacturers—the interests of commerce and industry.

The two men could not work together in the Cabinet. First Jefferson, then Hamilton, resigned during Washington's second term. Both men took their quarrels to the rest of the country, each seeking support for his policies.

The support came quickly. American citizens had fought a bitter war for their freedom, for this new idea of a democratic republic. They firmly believed that they should have a say in how the country was run. Federalist and Democratic-Republican groups were organized in many states. The groups took on the appearance of national parties as the country prepared for its third presidential election.

George Washington refused to run for a third term in 1796. That year the presidential election was a party contest between a Federalist, John Adams, and a Democratic-Republican, Thomas Jefferson.

Our Two-Party System

Since that year, the United States has always had two major political parties fighting to win the Presidency. The parties, their names, and their policies

have changed.* But in every presidential campaign, there have been two major parties—each trying to convince the voters to support its candidate.

The parties' fight for presidential power has not divided the country as the founding fathers feared it might. Actually, our early political parties did much to unite the various states. A workingman in a Northern city lived a very different life from that of a Southern farmer. Each might even want different kinds of laws to benefit his own section of the country. National politics pulled them together, though they disagreed on many local issues. As members of the same national party, they had to be willing to compromise on certain questions that affected the entire country.

This is still true today. Within each major party there are people from many different sections, holding many different opinions. There is one faction that is opposed to changes; its members might be called the "standpatters." There is also an opposing group of "experimenters," eager to try new plans and policies. And between these two groups there is a center faction that might be labeled "middle-of-the-roaders."

These factions in a political party can work together only by making compromises with each other. This

* Jefferson's Democratic-Republicans later became Democrats. Hamilton's Federalist party became disorganized and died out; its place in our two-party system was taken first by Whigs and eventually by today's Republicans.

arrangement often puzzles people in other countries.*
But the give-and-take within each American party
helps to unite the country; our two-party system does
work for us.

Our compromising parties fit in with our American
government. The Constitution divided power among
our three branches of government: the Presidency, the
Congress, and the Courts. This division of power created what we call a government of checks and bal-
ances. Each branch tends to act as a brake on the
others. Such a government makes compromises necessary; otherwise the government would come to a
standstill. The politicians of our two parties, accus-
tomed to compromise within their parties, help to
bring about the necessary compromises.

Only once in our history has our balancing, compromising two-party system broken down. That happened during the 1850's when the nation divided
sharply on the slavery issue. Neither party could con-
tain within itself both proslavery and antislavery
groups. Two clear-cut parties emerged; each stood
firmly for or against slavery. Lacking parties that were
willing to compromise, the nation faced a crisis that
led to a war between the states, the Civil War.

* In many countries, the political system is based on a number
of smaller parties, rather than on two major parties. With such a system, each party usually stands for a fairly definite set of ideas. People
who are used to such a system wonder why Americans do not have
one party for all the standpatters, another for the middle-of-the-
roaders, still another for the experimenters.

Some historians say that it may be the memory of this bitter war that keeps Americans today content with the fuzzy, overlapping outlines of our two major parties. It's safer, we may feel, to have standpatters and experimenters battling it out within each party than to risk a head-on collision between two parties with firmly opposed, uncompromising policies.

And so we see Republican politicians battling among themselves and Democrats doing the same. One kind of party battle occurs during the presidential primaries and state conventions. A follow-up battle is fought during the party's national nominating convention.

4

Act Two...
The Nomination of
Candidates

One warm summer evening you will flip on your television set and find that your favorite programs have been crowded off the screen. No cartoons, no secret agents, no comedians, no baseball games. Instead you will see a huge meeting of Republicans or Democrats gathered to choose their candidate for the Presidency. This is a national nominating convention.

For four or five days the country's television cameras will beam convention scenes into your living room. Thousands of delegates, visitors, reporters jam into the convention auditorium. There are rousing speeches, giddy parades, suspenseful votes. Crowds push through the packed lobby of the convention's headquarters hotel. Everywhere, smiling posters . . .

enthusiastic slogans (JOIN UP WITH JOHANSEN
. . . I'M HERE FOR REVERE . . . WIN WITH
WEBBER . . . BOWL 'EM OVER WITH BOYLE)
. . . and endless pictures of Democratic donkeys or
Republican elephants.

As you watch, you see American history being
made. History-in-the-making is never simple, and an
American political convention is a complicated affair
indeed.

Because of its noise, confusion, famous names,
crowds, booming ballyhoo, the nominating convention has often been compared to a three-ring circus.
But it is much more than a huge, lively show. During
these few hectic days a man will be chosen who may
be the next President of the United States.

How he is chosen might be summed up very simply:
The delegates cast their votes to choose among all the
possible candidates. The man who wins a majority of
the votes becomes the party's presidential candidate.

But that simple summary doesn't begin to explain
the political battles that will be fought here before the
big decision is made. The final decision on a candidate
must be a compromise; many different factions are
working against each other at this convention of party
members.

You'll catch only brief glimpses of the political battling on your television screen. Most of these maneu-
vers go on behind closed doors where no television

cameras can go. A look at the people gathered here will help you to understand what's going on backstage as you watch this three-ring circus.

The Key People

The convention will be called to order on Monday, and the sessions will continue until Thursday or Friday. During the weekend before the convention begins, you may see a special television news program previewing the convention's activities. The television reporter is standing in a crowded hotel lobby saying:

> We're talking to you this hot Saturday afternoon from the convention's headquarters hotel. The city is already jammed with convention visitors . . . and this hotel is a magnet that draws them all. Stand here long enough and you'll see most of the candidates hurrying to and from their headquarters . . . you'll overhear hundreds of delegates speaking with southern accents, western drawls, New England twangs . . . you'll be jostled by dozens of well-known politicians. . . .

With those comments, you've been introduced to the three most important groups at this convention: the *candidates*, the *voting delegates*, and the *delegation leaders*.

There may be six or eight or even ten *candidates* for the presidential nomination. Here are several men who won in the primaries and several who avoided the primaries; all of them spent the spring months campaigning and seeking support. Here, too, are a few who tossed their hats into the ring only recently; they hope to pick up support at the convention. There may even be one or two men who have not publicly announced that they are seeking the nomination; their supporters hope to **draft** them.

At least one thousand men and women here—and perhaps as many as three thousand—are *voting delegates*. These are the people who were chosen in the primary elections and at state conventions. They are active party members—many amateur politicians and some full-time professionals—who represent the party organizations in their own states. The delegates are divided into state groups; they work and vote in state delegations.*

---

* Each party has a rather complicated formula that determines how many votes each state's delegation will have. The formulas allot votes based mainly on a state's population, and on how well the party did within the state in the most recent state and national elections. At both parties' conventions, there are also non-state delegations from the District of Columbia, Puerto Rico, and the Virgin Islands; at the Democratic convention, Guam and the Canal Zone have delegations too.

Democratic conventions are always larger than Republican conventions because each state is allowed to divide its votes. A Democratic state organization may send twice as many delegates as it has votes; then each delegate will have only ½ vote.

At the Democratic national convention of 1964, for instance, there were 2,316 votes spread among 2,944 delegates and 108 national committeemen; the delegations ranged in size from 3 to 179. But at the Republicans' 1964 convention, there were 1,308 delegates, and each delegate had one full vote; the smallest delegation had 3 votes, the largest had 92. At each party's convention, the winning candidate needs one more than half of the total votes.

In each delegation, a few people stand out; they are the party's well-known politicians. Some may be Governors and Senators whose names are familiar throughout the country. Others may be national committeemen, or state chairmen who run the party organizations in their own states. These professional politicians are the *delegation leaders*.

From now until Wednesday these three key groups will be working hard to arrange the convention's big decision. At Wednesday's session the delegates will begin voting on a presidential candidate. You'll see the delegates sitting in stage groups in the convention auditorium. You'll hear the delegations cast their votes for the candidate they have chosen.

What you can't see is the behind-the-scenes activity that goes on far from the convention hall. This activity has begun already, is going on right now, in offices throughout the headquarters hotel and in other nearby hotels.

Each candidate is trying to persuade delegates to vote for him; each is speaking with delegation leaders who may be able to win over their delegates. Every delegate is trying to decide which man should get his vote. And every delegation leader is trying to pick the winning candidate, hoping to jump on the **bandwagon** of the man who may become President.

The presidential nomination is not the convention's only job; much other party business will be attended to during convention sessions. Nor are the candidates and delegates the only groups at this convention. As many as thirty thousand people have gathered in this city.

There are over one thousand alternate delegates.* There are official guests. There are unofficial visitors, eager supporters of the candidates, who will ask for passes to the balcony seats in the convention hall. There are members of citizens' groups who hope to influence the candidates and delegates. There are perhaps five thousand reporters covering the convention for newspapers and magazines, for radio and television stations. And finally, there are the convention officials who are handling the details for this huge meeting; they must make the crowded schedule run smoothly.

What's on the convention schedule? The delegates must select a vice-presidential nominee as well as a presidential candidate. They must approve the party's **platform** for the election campaign. And they will hear and discuss many special committee reports on party activities.

But the convention highlight is the decision on the presidential candidate. And the key people to watch are the candidates, the voting delegates, and the delegation leaders.

* Each state may send one alternate delegate for every vote allotted to it. If a delegate cannot attend the convention, or does not appear at a particular session, his alternate votes in his place.

How the Candidates Work

Our television camera is set up here in the hotel corridor outside Governor Boyle's campaign headquarters. Inside, pretty girls wearing Boyle buttons are serving Sunday afternoon brunch to visiting delegates. We haven't seen the Governor, but his campaign managers are busy shaking hands and talking earnestly with the visitors. . . .

Each candidate's staff has been here for several weeks, preparing to meet the delegates. Each has set up an office in or near the headquarters hotel; in each office, up go banners and posters boosting the candidate. Out come bright campaign buttons, badges, and fancy hats that will be passed out to anyone willing to be a walking advertisement for the candidate. And down goes the welcome mat for the delegates.

Each candidate tries to convince delegates that his policies have the most appeal and are best for the party and the country. A party, remember, is divided into different factions that disagree on many important issues.

Each campaign manager works hard to persuade delegates that his man is most popular with the voters and can win the election. The party is searching for a strong, attractive man who will appeal to independent voters as well as party members. A candidate must look like a popular winner if he hopes to persuade delegates to vote for him. This is the reason for the smiling posters, the enthusiastic slogans, the big campaign buttons.

With each candidate trying to look like a winner, the enthusiasm at a man's headquarters is no indication of his strength at the convention. Much more important is this question: How many votes can each man count on when Wednesday's balloting begins?*

The answer to that question determines a candidate's strategy at the convention. A man who is certain of many votes will plan one kind of convention strategy; a man with fewer votes will work differently.

The *front-runners* are the strongest candidates. These two or three men are sure of the votes of certain state delegations. Victories in the primaries may make a man a front-runner; he now has many delegates pledged to vote for him. Success at state conventions may make another man a front-runner; these states' delegates have been instructed to vote for him.

Each front-runner hopes to win the nomination on the first ballot. That is probably his best chance, for if no man wins a majority on that first vote, a second roll

* No one can be absolutely certain of the final answer. Many delegates have not decided how they will vote; some delegations may not publicly announce their voting plans. But everyone at the convention is making guesses and spreading rumors: "Tennessee's delegates are going for Webber!" "Illinois is split between Bonifant and Johansen!"

call will be necessary. Some delegates may shift their votes on this second ballot, and the front-runners may lose strength.* This is just what the weaker candidates are hoping for.

The *runners-up* are weaker candidates who cannot count on large blocks of votes, as the front-runners can. But a runner-up may gather strength on a second or third roll call.

He is often a middle-of-the-roader who appeals to many kinds of people; he may be the second choice of several different factions. If no front-runner wins a majority, even after several ballots, the delegates may compromise on a runner-up. Therefore this weaker candidate will have an advantage if he can convince some delegations to stall on the first ballot. One way of doing this is to nominate a favorite son.

Favorite sons are usually Governors, occasionally Senators; each is supported only by his own state's delegates. A favorite-son candidate will be nominated by his own delegation which will vote for him on the first ballot. Since a favorite son seldom expects to pick up additional votes from other states, his nomination is often just an honorary gesture to give the Governor or Senator national publicity.

But it may also be used as a special kind of conven-

---

* Pledges and instructions are not considered absolutely binding on delegates after the first ballot. If a candidate loses strength on the second or third roll call, his pledged delegates are usually free to switch their votes to another man.

tion strategy. If a delegation is stalling for time by making a favorite-son nomination, it waits to see which candidate will have the most strength on the first ballot. Each favorite son will be watched carefully, for when he pulls out of the race he may ask his delegation to vote for one of the front-runners or runners-up.

The *dark horses* bring up the rear. A **dark horse** candidate may not be well-known, but he does have a small group of loyal supporters. A dark horse has little hope unless many ballots go by with no leading candidate able to win a majority. If a convention is trapped in such a deadlock, a majority may be willing to accept a dark horse in an effort to reach agreement.

Not every convention, of course, will have this many candidates. Sometimes only one man is considered, for when the President is eligible for another term, his party usually renominates him if he wants to run. In the past 80 years, every President who wanted renomination has received it.*

The Democratic convention of 1964 gave the nomination to Lyndon B. Johnson, who had succeeded to the Presidency when John F. Kennedy was assassinated on November 22, 1963. Under the provisions of the Twenty-second Amendment to the Constitu-

---

* In 1884, the Republican convention denied renomination to President Chester A. Arthur. Several other Presidents were denied renomination before then, but none who wanted it has missed out on renomination since that time.

tion,* President Johnson will be eligible in 1968 to serve another full term.

How the Delegations Work

The crowd you see leaving that hotel conference room is the large New York delegation, which has just held its second caucus. With the convention due to open in a few hours, this Monday morning is meeting time for many delegations. . . . Now we'll try to get some word for you on how the New Yorkers have decided to vote. . . .

Soon after the delegates arrive, each delegation meets separately in **caucus** to discuss voting plans. Most delegations caucus frequently throughout the convention, for each state group wants the latest word on the voting strength of every candidate. Is any front-runner strong enough to win on the first ballot? Could their votes give him a majority? Or should they pin their hopes on a runner-up who may pull ahead later? How are the other delegations voting? Who is the second choice of most large delegations?

The delegation leaders are the ones who can answer these questions. These Governors, Senators, national committeemen, and state chairmen know many party leaders from every other state. Through their contacts, they can report on the positions of other delegations'

* The Twenty-second (or "two-term") Amendment states that no one may be *elected* to the Presidency more than twice. A man who has served no more than two years of another President's term, however, may still be elected to two full terms of his own.

leaders. They can give their delegates a clearer picture of what's really happening at this vast convention where New Yorkers or Floridians may not know Californians, Texans, and Iowans.

A delegation leader has a special stake in lining up with the winning candidate. He hopes the winner will be the candidate he prefers. But he's willing to go along with a second choice if he can have a hand in deciding who that compromise candidate will be. For above all he wants to be on the side of the party's nominee. If the man he supports should reach the White House, he himself might be appointed by the new President to an important government job.

At its first caucus, each delegation chooses one of its leaders to be chairman. This job is important, since the chairman speaks for the delegation on the convention floor and runs his delegation's caucuses. He may influence his delegates' voting decisions; he is most likely to be approached by the vote-seeking candidates and their managers. The delegation chairman is a link between the candidates and the average delegate.

Who is this average delegate, and how does he make his decision? He—or she—may be an amateur politician: a precinct committeeman, a county chairman. Or he may be an officeholder: a Congressman, a state legislator, a mayor, a county commissioner, a sheriff. He is pulled in many directions as he tries to decide which man will get his vote.

As a citizen, the delegate wants a man who will be a good President, a wise man who can lead the country well. Here he is influenced by his own judgment of what each candidate stands for. He would like to vote for a man whose political ideas are close to his own.

As a loyal Republican or Democrat, he wants a popular candidate, a man who can win the election for his party. Here he is influenced by primaries and public-opinion polls, and by the convention ballyhoo.

As a New Hampshireman or an Oregonian or a Missourian, he wants a man who will understand and sympathize with the special problems of his part of the country. In talking with the candidates' managers, he tries to learn which men favor laws that would solve those problems and benefit his own state.

As a member of his state delegation, he is influenced by the chairman and other delegation leaders. He depends on their reports of what is going on behind the scenes. And he knows that if he does not vote as they urge him to, their doors may be closed to him when he asks their help in the future.

Each delegate considers many angles before deciding how to vote. Each delegation leader hurries to many meetings—with leaders from other states, with candidates or their managers—before reporting back to his delegation. Each candidate consults his managers and his supporters in every delegation, carefully tallying the votes he can count on.

The delegations vote in caucus, choosing among

the candidates. Some states vote unanimously for one candidate; other delegations divide their votes among a number of candidates.*

The caucusing, the private meetings and conferences, continue throughout Monday and Tuesday. All this goes on behind the scenes while committee reports and other business are being discussed on the convention floor. But when Wednesday's nominating session opens, every delegate is in his seat in the convention hall.

The Nominations

> Governor Thomas Boyle's name has just been placed in nomination . . . and this entire hall is in an uproar as Boyle's delegates stage the first demonstration of the convention. A brass band is parading across the floor, followed by cheering delegates waving signs and banners. Up in the balcony Boyle's people are going wild . . . clapping, stamping, roaring, and showering the floor with confetti. . . .

Before the balloting can begin, nominations must be made. The states are called on in alphabetical order, and each is given a chance to make a nomination. During this long process, the name of each presidential hopeful is placed in nomination.

Every nominating speech is the signal for a wild

---

* At Democratic conventions, some states vote under the unit rule. This rule directs the delegation to vote unanimously for the candidate who receives a majority vote in caucus.

and noisy demonstration. The chairman of the convention may rap his gavel for order, but he will be completely ignored—which will not surprise him at all.

In fact, these noisy demonstrations surprise no one. Each wild hullabaloo has been carefully planned in advance, from the well-polished nominating speech down to the last shred of confetti.

What, then, is the purpose of the demonstration? It's designed to give the impression that the candidate is a sure winner. If the delegates parade long enough, if the spectators shout loud enough, some wavering delegates may be carried away by the show. They may be convinced to shift their votes before the balloting begins; and these last-minute shifts may result in a majority for one candidate.

Obviously, at each convention only one of the wildly cheered candidates can be a winner. But every campaign manager operates on the theory that a long, loud demonstration just *might* win the nomination for his man. Managers have been known to plot elaborate tricks as well as demonstrations to sway the delegates. And sometimes the tricks have worked.

In 1860, Abraham Lincoln's campaign managers actually forged a large supply of gallery tickets so that their supporters could hold down all the vacant balcony seats. Historians say that Lincoln's wildly enthusiastic gallery support had a large part in winning the Republican nomination for him.

At another Republican convention, in 1940, the

galleries were packed by supporters of Wendell Willkie; for days they kept up a constant, deafening chant of "We want Willkie!" Huge piles of pro-Willkie telegrams were delivered, in bushel baskets, to delegates on the convention floor. Early in the convention Willkie had been considered little more than a dark horse. But he gained votes on each roll call, gradually pulling ahead of the front-runners, and he finally won the nomination on the sixth ballot.

Frequently, of course, the tricks and demonstrations fail. Backers of Adlai E. Stevenson tried unsuccessfully to stir up support for their man at the Democratic convention in 1960. Stevenson's staff had been given 125 demonstrators' passes, as had the other candidates. But the Stevenson people, on entering the hall, kept sending back their passes to eager fellow supporters waiting outside. Close to 500 shouting, chanting Stevenson demonstrators took over the floor before the guards discovered their trick. But most delegates were unmoved by this emotional demonstration. Stevenson received only a scattering of votes, and John F. Kennedy easily won the nomination on the first ballot.

The Balloting

All the candidates at this convention have finally been nominated. The delegates are back in their seats, waiting tensely for the roll call on the first ballot. In a moment you will hear the clerk of the convention call on Alabama. . . . There it is, and the Alabama chairman is rising to announce his delegation's vote. . . .

As the roll call moves slowly through the list of states, heading down toward Wisconsin and Wyoming, the big question is: "How close can each frontrunner come to a majority?"

If one candidate is very close when the roll call is completed, you may see a delegation chairman jump up and wave his state's sign. This is a signal that he wants to be recognized by the convention chairman; his delegation has decided to switch its votes from another candidate to the near-winner.

Those votes may be enough to give this candidate a majority. Now everyone knows that this man has the nomination. State signs will be waving on all sides of the hall; each delegation is fighting to be recognized so that it can switch to the winner. Everyone wants to jump aboard the winning bandwagon.

But if no one approaches a majority on the first ballot, another roll call will be started. If this second vote also falls short of a majority, suspense mounts. By now it may be late at night, even hours past midnight. Delegations will be caucusing right on the convention floor. Messengers hurry from one caucus to another as the delegates try to reach agreement.

The favorite sons are usually out of the running now; their delegates have switched to front-runners and runners-up. Any favorite son who is picking up unexpected support may become a dark horse if the balloting goes on long enough.

A front-runner who does not gain votes on each new ballot will find himself out of the race. Few delegations will continue to support a candidate who is falling behind.

If all the front-runners are losing ground, a majority of delegates may agree to compromise on a runner-up. Or the roll calls may go on and on, with delegations constantly shifting their votes, until a dark horse pulls up from behind.

However it happens, one candidate finally wins a majority, and the fight within the party is over. When the newly chosen presidential candidate makes his acceptance speech, at the convention's closing session, he stresses that the entire party must now unite for the election campaign. After months of battling and maneuvering among themselves, the party's factions traditionally join forces to convince the voters that the Republican, or Democratic, candidate is on his way to the White House.

Occasionally, these opposing groups within a party cannot bring themselves to unite for the campaign. If they have been deeply divided on a very important issue before and during the convention, the quarreling factions may not be able to smooth over their differences.

During the past few decades, the question of civil rights has been one of the most serious faced by our country, and it has created great problems within both political parties. In 1948, a group of Southern Democrats walked out of the Democratic convention because they strongly opposed the civil rights position taken by the party and the party's newly nominated candidate, President Harry S. Truman. Calling themselves States' Rights Democrats, but nicknamed Dixiecrats, they nominated their own presidential and vice-presidential candidates and ran a campaign of their own.

Again in 1964, the civil rights issue created disunity in the Republican party. A number of important Republicans—including some Governors and Senators—were so opposed to the civil rights position of the Republican presidential candidate, Barry M. Goldwater, that they did not work for him during the campaign; some even refused to appear with him in public when he campaigned in their states.

The Vice-Presidential Candidate

The convention delegates cannot go home after the presidential nomination; a vice-presidential candidate is still to be chosen. The balloting for this nomination is seldom exciting because traditionally the presidential candidate makes known to the convention his choice of a running mate, and the delegates nominate this man.*

The presidential candidate usually has two goals in mind when he thinks about a man to share the party's ticket with him. One is to attract support from additional voters who may not strongly favor his own candidacy. This he does by seeking a man different from himself, someone from a different section of the country, someone with different ideas about government. Another goal is to unify the party for the campaign; and this he does by seeking a man from a different faction within the party, a faction that may have bitterly opposed his own nomination.

John F. Kennedy's choice of Lyndon B. Johnson for the vice-presidential nomination at the 1960 Democratic convention is a fair example of both these goals. Johnson had been Kennedy's leading challenger for the presidential nomination, and he had the support of many delegates. In naming Johnson as his running mate, Kennedy brought their two factions together for the campaign. Also, as a Texan, Johnson was expected to strengthen the Democratic ticket in states where Kennedy, an Easterner, needed help in winning votes.

---

* One notable exception: In 1956, the Democratic convention was astonished when Adlai Stevenson, who had just been nominated as the presidential candidate, refused to name his preference for a running mate. Instead, he threw the nomination for Vice President open to the entire convention, which named Estes Kefauver.

The Platform

Early in the convention, before nominating the party's candidates, the delegates must agree on a platform. This is a statement of the party's policies.

Each **plank** in the platform tells where the party stands on an important problem facing the nation. What should be done about the war in Vietnam? Should changes be made in our foreign policy, in the draft laws, in our space program? Can taxes be lowered? What should the government do about civil rights, about unemployment, about poverty, about slum clearance, about air pollution, about education?

Answers to such questions are hammered out by a committee which then presents the platform to the delegates. The platform committee holds public hearings before the convention opens. To these hearings come members of many citizens' organizations. The people in each organization are trying to promote certain public policies in which they believe. These organizations are called **pressure groups,** or special-interest groups.

There are representatives from farmers' organizations, from businessmen's groups, from labor unions. From civil liberties organizations and teachers' committees and veterans' organizations and women's clubs and doctors' associations and youth groups.

Each group wants a special kind of help for its

members. Each representative argues for a plank supporting his group's policies. This is a sort of horse-trading arrangement. Each representative is suggesting, "If your platform includes a plank favoring our policies, our members are likely to vote for your party."

The platform committee wants to offer something to everyone. But since many of the special-interest groups oppose each other, no plank can be made too definite or strong; it might offend another group.

Furthermore, the platform must also satisfy many opposing factions within the party itself; a majority of delegates will have to approve every plank. If any plank is too strong, delegates who oppose it may fight against it on the convention floor; and the platform committee is anxious to avoid floor fights.

The platform, therefore, is usually a vague document that is just barely acceptable to everyone. A standard political joke points out that while a platform is supposed to show where a party stands, it's seldom strong enough for a candidate to run on.

A presidential candidate really creates his own platform in his campaign speeches. His opinions on important issues usually influence the voters far more than the platform does.

5

A Backward Glance ...
at Presidential
Nominations

Today we take for granted the crowds of delegates, the noise, the ballyhoo of our nominating conventions. But these scenes would surely puzzle the men who planned our government.

Those first Americans did not nominate their presidential candidates as today's Democrats and Republicans do. Since the Constitution says nothing about how candidates shall be nominated, the early parties were free to experiment with various methods. Our nominating system has developed through the trial-and-error of everyday, practical politics.

In the beginning there were no huge gatherings of delegates who represented party members in every state. Instead, presidential candidates were chosen by a handful of the country's leaders. Most of the founding fathers believed that presidential nominations were the responsibility of the men who ran the national government.

The early American Presidents—Washington, Adams, Jefferson, Madison, Monroe—were nominated by Congressional caucuses. The caucus was a meeting of each party's members in Congress. Each Congressional caucus selected its party's candidate. The first caucuses were secret meetings; but after a few presidential elections these Congressional nominating sessions began attracting much public attention. They were criticized by citizens and by newspapers in many states.

At this time the young country was growing larger. Pioneers moved out into new territories; new leaders appeared in these frontier areas. These leaders were popular with their own neighbors, although they might not be well-known among the Senators and Congressmen who gathered in the nation's capital. Citizens in all the states felt that their own local leaders were worthy of becoming national leaders, perhaps even presidential candidates.

Each state's politicians began to ask, "Why should Congressional caucuses make presidential nominations?" They argued that the Constitution gave the states the right to run elections; therefore the party leaders in the states should help to choose presidential candidates.

So during the early 1800's the state party organizations tried new ways of nominating presidential candidates. By 1824, the Congressional caucus had almost disappeared. In some states, each party would call a meeting of its local leaders to nominate candidates. In other states, the legislatures would make nominations.

It soon became confusing to have presidential nominations coming from so many separate states. Finally both major parties called for nationwide nominating conventions. These meetings would be attended by party leaders from all the states. In 1831 and 1832, the first national nominating conventions were held to select candidates for the 1832 election.

Those meetings set today's pattern. For more than 135 years, our presidential candidates have been chosen at national conventions.

Presidential primaries were a later experiment, an attempt to bring even more party members into the nominating process. In the early 1900's, many reformers claimed that nominating conventions were controlled by a small group of political bosses who ran the parties' organizations in the large cities. Convention delegates from these cities voted as their bosses directed. The reformers urged their states to hold primary elections in which party members could show which presidential candidate they preferred. Then delegates would go to the conventions pledged to support a man chosen by the local party members, not by the party boss. Although presidential primaries were accepted by fewer than one-third of the states, their influence has been—and still is—widespread.

As you look back, you can retrace the road that presidential nominations followed. The nominating process started with a few national leaders in Congress. It spread out to include party leaders in the various states. Finally, with the primaries, it reached out to millions of party members throughout the country.

How Convention Campaigning Has Changed

Primary elections had another effect on the nominating process. These pre-convention battles opened the way for much earlier and more active campaigning by the men seeking the parties' nominations.

Throughout the 1800's, a man who wanted the nomination rarely tossed his own hat into the ring. He took a much more dignified approach. The presidential hopeful stood on the sidelines as his backers built up support for him. In theory, at least, he bided his time and waited to be drafted by his party.

Even at the convention, his campaign manager did all the work of seeking out votes. For one hundred years after the first conventions in the 1830's, candidates never appeared at conventions unless they happened to be attending as delegates.

In fact, the winner did not officially learn of his nomination until as long as a month after the convention. Then a committee formally visited him to present the news. This odd custom ended in 1932, when Franklin D. Roosevelt flew to the Democratic convention in Chicago to accept the nomination on the spot. After that, more and more presidential hopefuls attended conventions and campaigned there actively.

Since then the successful candidate's acceptance speech has become the dramatic close of each convention. This is the signal for the party to end its squabbling and prepare to battle against the opposing party.

A Summing-up

As the delegates leave the convention city, as janitors sweep up the red-white-and-blue litter in the convention hall, reporters are writing newspaper articles and television scripts analyzing what happened during those four or five frenzied days. When you read and hear these comments, you will discover many arguments for and against the convention system.

You may even hear some political experts insist that these national nominating conventions should be abolished. What are the reasons for this viewpoint?

1. The conventions are disorganized and un-

dignified. The circus atmosphere does not allow for serious discussion of candidates and platform issues.

2. The conventions have no legal standing. They have merely grown through experiments and customs. There are no Federal laws regulating conventions and the state laws for selecting delegates are all different.

3. The conventions are too large. Most delegates have little opportunity to exchange opinions with people from other states. In larger delegations many people do not even know one another. This concentrates power in the hands of a small group of political leaders.

4. Too much goes on behind the scenes. It's too easy for deals to be made by campaign managers and delegation leaders who may control the convention.

5. The delegation leaders are too concerned with picking a winner. They do not search conscientiously for a man who will use presidential power wisely. Instead they ask practical political questions like these: Do the opinion polls show that he is popular throughout the country? Is he a safe candidate who has not antagonized any large groups of voters? Will he go along with our ideas of how the party and the country should be run?

These are strong arguments. But on the other side there are strong arguments in favor of our convention system:

1. The convention pulls together the fifty state or-

ganizations. Between presidential elections, each state's party organization operates independently. Only once in four years does the party become a truly national organization.

2. The convention provides a meeting place for a cross section of party members, local politicians as well as national leaders. It creates enthusiasm for the presidential campaign.

3. The convention gives the voters an opportunity to watch the would-be candidates in action. The voters can form opinions of how each man might perform in a crisis.

4. The convention helps voters to discover which group within the party has the most strength. Since each party is made up of various factions, it's valuable for the country to see the tug-of-war among them. Voters can evaluate what the party really stands for.

5. Sometimes the convention does air important national issues. Occasionally there will be a showdown fight on the convention floor over some plank in the platform. This is healthy for the party and valuable for the voters.

6. How else could presidential nominations be made? If the nominations came from the states, how would the entire party finally reach agreement on just one man?

Perhaps this last argument is the most convincing one. As you have seen, American parties did experiment with various methods before they finally turned to national conventions for nominating presidential candidates.

For all the arguments against them, conventions are an accepted part of American politics. The political experts may continue to point out the disadvantages of our nominating system. But most do agree that it has given us some great Presidents, many competent Presidents, and only a scattering of men who were not strong and wise enough to lead the country effectively.

6

Act Three . . .
The Campaign

Early September always spells back-to-school and back-to-work. Slowly the country pulls itself out of its vacation mood.

But in a presidential election year the tempo accelerates; little time is wasted looking back at vacation memories. There is too much to look forward to as campaign excitement spreads across the country.

The two presidential candidates take to the road, making speeches, shaking hands, seeking votes. Every newspaper carries headlines reporting the candidates' activities. Billboards sprout along the highways, urging citizens to "VOTE REPUBLICAN!" . . . "GO DEMOCRATIC!" On a thousand Main Streets, busy party workers turn empty stores into local campaign headquarters, decorating the windows with posters and red-white-and-blue banners. Men and

women, boys and girls, decorate their jackets with
buttons announcing, "I'M BOOSTING BOYLE" ...
"I WANT WEBBER."

Millions of Americans are asking, "Which man
are you voting for?"

Thousands of other Americans are working day
and night to swing the votes to their candidates.

The campaign workers are trying to reach the voters, and the voters are trying to decide between the two
candidates. The working and the deciding monopo-
lize the country's attention from Labor Day in
September until Election Day in November.

Top-Level Strategy

Webber Hits Hard on Foreign Policy in Tour Through East

ALBANY, Sept. 10—Senator
Charles Webber attacked the Administration's foreign policy in his
first major campaign speech as . . .

Boyle Says U.S. Economy Is on Big Up-Swing

MILWAUKEE, Sept. 12—Defend-
ing the Administration's domestic
policy in his opening speech of the
presidential campaign, Governor
Thomas Boyle said that . . .

What to say? Where and when to say it? These are the big questions facing each candidate and his top-level staff, the advisers and friends who help plan his campaign strategy.

WHAT TO SAY? In speeches and interviews each candidate will tell how he would solve the nation's troubling problems.

How should the government handle foreign policy —defense plans, atomic testing, United Nations, foreign aid, the war in Vietnam? What should the government do about domestic policy—taxes, unemployment, anti-poverty programs, education, civil rights, slum clearance? These questions are the issues of the campaign, the problems most voters will consider and argue about for the next two months.

Always, the candidate whose party has held the Presidency for the past four years will defend his party's four-year record; the other candidate will attack that record. Beyond this, each man will play up certain issues, his party's strong points: the policies he considers likely to gain most votes for him. This means that often the two men will be talking at cross-purposes; one will hammer away at certain issues which the other avoids.

WHERE TO SAY IT? The fact that voters live in fifty separate states plays a large part in mapping out the candidate's traveling plans.

The candidate tries to visit every state, but he and

his staff must make top-strategy decisions about which states will see more of him. In which states is he strongest? He must visit them to solidify his position; he cannot take their votes for granted. Which states are good possibilities, but not at all certain? He must work even harder there to pull their votes into his column.

You might think that in a national election, state boundaries would fade away as each party unites in a great effort to campaign for its presidential candidate. This does not happen; instead, each state must put on its own individual campaign. A candidate, looking at a map of the nation, sees fifty separate groups of votes. Because of the way we vote, state boundaries are all-important in a presidential campaign. As we shall see, on Election Day the real voting power is concentrated within state borders.

This is why the candidates probe to find their weak spots. By plane and train, the two men cross back and forth over the country, seizing every opportunity to make additional visits to those doubtful states.

WHEN TO SAY IT?   The campaign starts big, but it must wind up even bigger.

Each candidate wants to catch and keep the voters' interest for two long months. Each man's campaign is planned to build up to the climax of Election Day. Thus, both candidates will save some of their most dramatic plans, their strongest attacks, for the last few weeks.

National, State, and Local Campaigns

> ## National Chairman
> ## Says Party Builds
> ## Local Strength
>
> WASHINGTON, Sept. 16—Local Republican clubs in every state are gaining a new lease on life under the impetus of the presidential election, according to Republican National Chairman Peter Ogden . . .
>
> ———

While the candidate and his close advisers criss-cross the country, a huge army of party workers goes into action. Party groups from the National Committee down to the precinct committees join in the electioneering.

THE NATIONAL LEVEL. The national chairman, chosen by the candidate, works in Washington. He directs the entire coast-to-coast campaign. The national chairman's staff handles countless big jobs and small details: raising campaign funds; planning television programs; issuing press releases; deciding when to attack and when to defend; writing campaign pamphlets about the candidate and the party; enlisting the party's politicians to make speeches in every state. Above all, the national chairman must persuade all the state and local party groups to pull togethe for the national ticket. When you remember that these groups may have been bitterly divided at the nominating convention, you can realize what a difficult job this is.

THE STATE LEVEL.   In Iowa, Nevada, Illinois, Kentucky, and all points east and west, each party's state chairman is working overtime.

He must know what is going on nationally as well as within his own state. He must tie in the national strategy with the campaigns of his own state and local candidates. He and his staff must raise money, plan publicity, keep up the enthusiasm of the county chairmen. The state organization depends on the county and local units to bring out large, cheering crowds when the presidential candidate tours the state.

THE LOCAL LEVEL.   The local campaign headquarters is the busiest spot on Main Street during September and October.

When the headquarters office is opened, new workers are recruited to handle the dozens of jobs that must be done to reach the voters. Phone calls must be made to set up committees, to plan rallies and picnics, coffee hours and parties. Envelopes must be addressed, stuffed with pamphlets, and mailed to voters. Most important, canvassers must try to visit every home in the area to discuss their candidate and the issues, in an effort to win votes. They also hope to raise money for the local campaign by asking supporters for contributions. The campaign jobs add up and multiply in party headquarters in each small town, in each corner of every county, in each neighborhood of every city.

Organizations—and Confusion

Statewide Volunteer Group for Boyle Sets Up Headquarters Here

BOSTON, Sept. 20—The formation of a Massachusetts "Volunteers for Boyle" group was announced today by F. John Finley, co-chairman of the organization . . .

The party organizations are not the only ones working in the campaign. Temporary groups are set up to electioneer for each candidate: "Volunteers for Boyle," "Citizens for Webber." Each group organizes local committees in every state, trying to spread an active network into many cities, large and small.

Other campaign committees are often organized by special interest groups, designed to appeal to certain large groups of voters: "Businessmen for Webber," "Women for Boyle," "Farmers for Webber," "Labor for Boyle," "Young People for Webber," "Lawyers for Boyle," "Doctors for Webber." What is the need for such groups?

Some citizens want to work for a candidate but will

not work in a political party. Some voters seem more willing to listen to volunteers from these nonparty groups than to the parties' precinct workers. And these groups set up just for the election are very effective for raising money that is needed to run the campaign.

Sometimes the formation of these groups may be a publicity move, to give the impression that the candidate has great support from many different **blocs** of voters. Actually, the members in each bloc are usually divided—some working for one candidate and some for the other—so they tend to cancel each other out.

There is no limit to the number of party organizations and citizens' committees that may be working to elect a President. But in all the confusion of organizing, the parties never forget that the individual voter is their target. What happens when voter meets party on the precinct level?

Getting Out the Vote

Both Parties Push To Get Out Vote; Large Turnout Seen

WASHINGTON, Sept. 25—With both Republicans and Democrats working hard on their respective get-out-the-vote drives, political leaders here predict a record turnout on Election Day . . .

Michigan Precinct Leader Tells How, Why He Does Job

DETROIT, Sept. 27—Jim Lewitt is an auto worker at a nearby plant, but his big job these days is working as a precinct captain. Between now and Election Day, every spare minute of his time will be spent canvassing voters in his own neighborhood . . .

The precinct captain is explaining to the reporter how he covers the big job he has lined up for himself between now and Election Day.

"There are 593 voters in my neighborhood precinct," he says, "and I'm going to visit every one of them at least once. My job is to round up as many votes as possible for my candidate, from among those 593 people.

"I make out a file card for every voter I visit, write his name and address and voting preference. Some people don't like to tell you how they're voting; but usually I can judge what their thinking is. Actually, most people have already made up their minds.

"I find that voters divide into three groups—those who are definitely against us, those who are definitely for us, and those who are undecided. The ones who are against us, I thank and cross off my list; there's no point wasting my time or theirs by arguing or planning to visit them again. The ones who are definitely for us, I thank briefly and check on my list. I'll remind them they must be **registered** so they can vote; and on Election Day, I'll make sure they get to the polls.

"The undecideds are the ones I usually spend the most time with. If they ask me why I'm for Webber, I tell them, with facts and figures. I usually leave some campaign pamphlets with them, and I remind them about registering, too. Later in the campaign I'll go back to answer any new questions they may have, but I won't do a high-pressure selling job. Most people would resent that.

"That's a lot of visiting and talking, but it pays off on Election Day. I've heard people say, 'Just one vote more or less won't matter.' But they're wrong; every vote counts. A few years ago, I ran in a primary myself. I tried to get the nomination for the state legislature. I lost by 140 votes in a district with 144 precincts. Just one more vote in each precinct and I would have won the nomination!"

Throughout the country—in every precinct of every city and town—other party workers are ringing doorbells, making file cards, keeping records of their voters. By late September, both parties have a rough idea of how many people are firmly on their side and of how many others they hope to persuade.

Politicians and public-opinion polls estimate that as few as ten or fifteen per cent of the voters may still be undecided as the campaign heads into October. These are the people who can swing the election one way or the other. As that precinct captain demonstrated, every vote does count. And as we shall see, because of our particular way of electing a President, just a handful of votes in the right state can spell victory or defeat for a candidate.

These, then, are the twin goals of each candidate: First, to keep up the enthusiasm of the faithful party supporters and get them out to vote on Election Day. Second, to find and win over the undecided voters who may swing the election. These are also the goals of every campaign worker, from the top-level staffs to the men and women on Main Street.

Reaching the Voters

By October, both candidates are moving at top speed. How do these two men make contact with the tens of millions of people who will choose between them? In today's fast-moving world, facts and opinions speed through many channels—newspapers and news magazines, polls, television. Each channel presents opportunities and creates problems for the candidate.

NEWSPAPERS AND NEWS MAGAZINES. Both men must keep their names in the headlines; to get coverage, they must make news constantly. Day and night they speak at meetings and at press conferences which are reported by the dozens of newsmen traveling with them from state to state.

Newspapers do more than report the news. They also comment on it. During the campaign most papers endorse one candidate or the other.

Nation's Papers Back Webber by 2-to-1 Count

CHICAGO, Oct. 10—A nation-wide survey indicates that more than two-thirds of the country's newspapers are giving editorial support to the candidacy of Senator Charles Webber . . .

A newspaper will use its editorial page to explain— in editorials and in political cartoons—why it supports one candidate, and why it expects and hopes that he will win the election. This may create quite a stir in the town or city where the paper is published, especially if the paper comes out for a candidate whose party it has not supported in the past. A newspaper can often win votes for a candidate if readers agree with and respect the policies of the paper.

Sometimes, editors may do more to promote their candidates: a paper may give the biggest headlines, the best news space to the man it supports. It may even slant the news of its candidate's activities, playing up his successful appearances and playing down those that are not enthusiastically received.

News magazines often have even more influence than newspapers because they reach so many more voters. Usually a daily paper is read in only one city or area, and it is soon thrown away. But one issue of a magazine is read by many millions of people from coast to coast, and each magazine is saved for many days, or even weeks, in people's homes, in libraries, in doctors' waiting rooms.

POLLS. Throughout the campaign, public-opinion polls checks the voters' attitudes. Some polls try to predict the outcome of the election. Others test the popularity of a candidate's stand on certain issues.

Gallup Poll Shows Boyle Leads Webber by 4.3 Per Cent

PRINCETON, Oct. 16—Among voters who are definitely committed to one candidate or the other, Governor Thomas Boyle is leading by 4.3 per cent, according to the latest national survey conducted by the Gallup Poll . . .

Do polls influence the voters? They often do, but it is almost impossible to predict how this influence will affect an election. Poll results sometimes lose votes for a candidate who looks like a sure winner because some of his supporters may feel they need not bother to vote. The polls may also take votes away from the weaker candidate; wavering supporters may decide that they would be wasting their votes on a man who has no chance of winning. On the other hand, poll results may actually help the weaker candidate by making his supporters more determined to work harder and win more backing for him.

Polls can influence candidates, too. If a poll shows that a candidate's stand on some issue is misunderstood or unpopular, he may make greater efforts to persuade voters that he is right. Or he may decide to shift his position to a more popular stand.

TELEVISION.   This newest channel of communication offers the candidate a vast audience.

---

30 Million View Webber Speech on Television

LOS ANGELES, Oct. 20—Television network officials estimate that an audience of close to 30 million people tuned in on Senator Charles Webber's televised appearance at the Hollywood Bowl . . .

His speeches are televised; he appears on interview and discussion programs. He makes brief films that are shown, like commercials, between regular programs throughout the day and evening. Millions of viewers are exposed to him constantly.

Television allows the candidate to get his message directly to the voters. He need not worry that an unsympathetic reporter or editor may cut out or distort some of his statements.

But television raises problems, too, and making a TV speech on a national hookup is much like walking a tightrope. The candidate must discuss national issues which will interest all of his listeners—but he must talk in general terms that will appeal to different kinds of people in many different areas. He knows that people want a President to be a strong, capable leader—but when he speaks to the entire nation at once he may hesitate to express strong opinions for fear of offending large blocs of voters.

He is very much aware of the picture he presents on the TV screen in each listener's living room; a candidate can actually win or lose because of the way he comes across on camera. Camera angles, shadows, even make-up can make one man seem more, or less, attractive than his opponent. This creates a problem, too, for the voters who may wonder whether they are seeing the man himself, or just the "image" of a candidate, created by TV directors, cameramen, and publicity advisers.

For the candidate, too, TV appearances may lack a flesh-and-blood feeling; he misses the opportunity to make a personal, human contact with his audience. He cannot judge their reactions to what he says, nor can he enjoy and respond to their mass enthusiasm.

THE PERSONAL TOUCH. To make real contact with the electorate, the candidate must get out of the television studio, out into the cities and towns where he can speak to local groups. Even in our mechanical age, there is no substitute for seeing and hearing a candidate in person. This can clinch the waverer's decision and can fire the party worker's determination to win more votes for his candidate.

There is more to this than the listener's emotional reaction to being near a famous man. When a candidate speaks to a local group, he can talk on issues of immediate interest to those particular people.

Huge Turnout for Pittsburgh Rally Encourages Boyle

PITTSBURGH, Oct. 25—An enthusiastic audience in this industrial city applauded Governor Thomas Boyle's strong pro-labor speech, convincing the Governor that he stands a good chance of carrying much of the labor vote . . .

Webber Pledges Tax Allowance to Oil Producers

SAN ANTONIO, Oct. 29—Reassuring local oil men that they could anticipate liberal tax allowances, Senator Charles Webber stated that . . .

He can talk farm prices to farmers, slum clearance to city dwellers. He can speak of flood control, irrigation projects, or highway construction in areas that need such help. These close-to-home issues are often the ones that finally sway voters. A citizen may realize that foreign policy decisions are urgent, but it's usually his own backyard that interests him most.

THE BALLYHOO. The candidates swing around the country, speaking at outdoor rallies and in auditoriums . . . driving in motorcades down Main Street and Broadway . . . shaking hands at clambakes, factories, state fairs . . . talking, talking, talking in Atlanta, Georgia, and Guthrie Center, Iowa; in Las Vegas, Nevada, and Burlington, Vermont . . . anyplace a big enough crowd can be collected.

Everywhere, there is the ballyhoo: the campaign pictures and slogans on lapel buttons (MY VOTE'S PINNED DOWN FOR BOYLE) . . . on bumper stickers (DRIVE AHEAD WITH WEBBER) . . . on matchbooks (STRIKE UP FOR BOYLE) . . . on chewing-gum wrappers (STICK WITH WEBBER). Always, for each candidate, there is the need to create the atmosphere of victory.

What of the Voters?

How do the voters react to the electioneering? Do they believe everything they read in the papers? Do the television speeches change their minds? Are they significantly influenced by the poll results, the volunteers who ring their doorbells, the campaign literature jamming their mailboxes? Are they impressed by the ballyhoo? That probably depends on the kinds of voters they are.

Some voters always support one party, election after election. Remember that four out of five Americans consider themselves either Democrats or Republicans. Their chosen party will usually get their votes no matter who the candidate is. In most campaigns, the hectic electioneering will only reassure the party regulars that their party's man is right for the country.

There are exceptions to this, of course; they usually occur when a candidate takes a very vigorous position on a deeply emotional issue. Then, even a party regular will desert his party if he disagrees strongly enough with the candidate's position. He may switch to the other party's candidate for this election, or he may support a third-party candidate if there is one, or he may stay home on Election Day.

Independent voters are not bound by party ties. Independents account for perhaps twenty per cent of the voting population. They're the ones who often hold the balance of power in a presidential election; but not all of them are swayed by the campaign. Some independents decided long before this election year which party they would support. They studied the politicians in action, watched to see which laws and policies each party supported and opposed.

Other independents are still undecided early in the campaign. The electioneering probably has most influence on these undecided independent voters. More and more of them find reasons for making up their minds as the campaign builds up.

To one voter, one certain issue may be all-important; he will choose the candidate whose stand is closest to his own viewpoint on this issue. Another voter may be most interested in a candidate's overall attitude toward government. He may want a man who believes in experiment and change; or he may prefer a man who will keep things as they are.

The personality of the candidate may be a deciding factor. A man's approach to solving problems, his way of thinking and expressing himself, affects voters. This is not simply a question of a citizen's asking, "Do I like this man?" But rather: "Do I feel I can rely on him? Will I feel secure with this man at the head of our government? Is he strong enough to solve the problems we face at home? Can he negotiate successfully with the Russians, the African nations, the French, the Chinese?"

One final deciding factor may be what is happening in the world during the last weeks of the campaign. If the news is good, it may prompt people to vote for the party in power; voters will feel that this party's policies have been successful. If the news is bad, the voters may decide that it's time to shift to the other party which will try a new approach.

Every voter reaches his decision by a different route. But each voter, somewhere along the line, is bound to ask himself: Which candidate is best qualified to lead the country? How will I feel with him in the White House?

7

A Backward Glance...
at Presidential Campaigns

Have presidential campaigns always been conducted as they are today? Yes and no. Except for our first two elections, when George Washington was everybody's choice, we have always had the party activity, the speeches, arguments, attacks and counterattacks. But there have been significant changes in the patterns of presidential campaigns.

You would not have felt at home during early campaigns; the different laws and customs would have seemed strange. Many citizens were not allowed to vote. There was no such thing as widespread national electioneering. And the people saw little of the presidential candidates. Why was this so?

To begin with, ideas about democracy and representative government were different then. The nation's leaders did not believe that everyone in a democratic republic should have an equal voice in running the government. Voting was considered a special privilege reserved for landowners; most states' election laws said that a man had to own a certain amount of property to be qualified to vote. At first, less than half the men in most states could vote; and women, of course, could not go to the polls.*

As for national electioneering—it was an impossibility. Even in spirited campaigns, the political activity was local. It had to be. Campaigners could not reach all the voters quickly and easily. There was no radio or television to carry speeches to every corner of the country. There were no planes—nor at first even trains—to speed campaigners through every state. There were no telephones or telegraphs to transmit news rapidly.

For the most part, the presidential campaign was carried on locally by each candidate's supporters. It was considered undignified for a candidate to **take the stump** in his own behalf. He might write letters to politicians, might confer privately with his backers, but he did little public electioneering. Throughout most of the nineteenth century, it simply was not the custom for the presidential candidates to take their arguments to the people.

Gradually, all three of these situations changed.

* American women received the right to vote in 1920, with the ratification of the Nineteenth Amendment to the Constitution.

How Campaigns Changed

Presidential electioneering changed because of new voting laws, broader political activity, new inventions, new campaign customs.

As new frontier states like Kentucky, Tennessee, Ohio, Indiana joined the original thirteen states, they enacted election laws allowing *all* adult male citizens to vote. The pioneers who settled these areas were used to running their own local affairs. When their territories became states, the citizens insisted that state election laws must not include property qualifications for voting.

Gradually, people without property in the older, Eastern states demanded that they, too, should have a voice in electing candidates. By the 1820's most states had abolished property qualifications. Democracy was growing stronger throughout the country.

Andrew Jackson's campaign in 1828 reflected these newer feelings about democracy. It was the first campaign organized on a truly national basis in an effort to reach the masses of voters.

Jackson, who was running against President John Quincy Adams, was the candidate of the plain people: the frontiersmen, the Western farmers, the Eastern workers. His supporters organized local committees throughout the twenty-four states to send campaign information to the newspapers and the voters. They planned political rallies in every village and city. Of course, their news could travel no faster than a horse could run; their political speakers could reach audiences only within the sound of their own voices. But the nationwide planning and organizing did reach the people: Jackson won the election.

The election of 1840 was the first one to introduce campaign ballyhoo. William Henry Harrison ran against President Martin Van Buren. Harrison's supporters were so divided among themselves that they could not even agree on a platform. Instead of talking about issues, they resorted to slogans, brass bands, parades, and blazing bonfires to attract attention. Harrison won; and this success may have set the pattern for the fast-moving booming campaigns that grew bigger and noisier every four years.

Then too, the invention of the telegraph early in 1844 helped to speed up the tempo of presidential campaigns. In fact, one of the first important messages sent by telegraph was the news of James Polk's nomination by the Democratic convention of 1844. This news traveled so rapidly over the newly installed telegraph wire from Baltimore to Washington that many people did not believe it. It was easy to disbelieve, because Polk had not been considered a leading presidential hopeful. He was the first dark horse to be nominated in the history of our country.

During the next two decades, a network of railroads

joined the telegraph in bringing together all sections of the growing country. In 1869 the first transcontinental rail line was completed. At last it was possible for campaigners to travel easily into every state. Some presidential candidates did begin to make limited speaking tours; but it was not until the end of the nineteenth century that coast-to-coast railroad campaigning came into its own.

It was in the campaign of 1896 that William Jennings Bryan originated the whistle-stop tour. He canvassed the nation by railroad, traveling 18,000 miles, stopping at dozens of depots every day to make speeches from the rear platform of his train. Bryan, who was famous as an orator, made 600 campaign speeches—an all-time record. On the other hand, his opponent William McKinley perfected the front-porch campaign. McKinley stayed home, received visiting delegations, shook their hands, said very little, and won the election.

Despite Bryan's defeat, whistle-stopping caught on as a campaign custom. After that, most candidates toured the country actively by train. But as late as 1920, Warren G. Harding conducted a successful front-porch campaign. And in 1924, President Calvin Coolidge, who had succeeded to the Presidency when President Harding died in 1923, was elected after a campaign in which he seldom left the White House.

In the 1920's, two more electioneering techniques

originated. The 1924 campaign saw both candidates making radio broadcasts to the nation. And in 1928, motorcades were introduced by both Herbert Hoover and Alfred E. Smith.

In 1932, Franklin D. Roosevelt conducted a grass-roots campaign, making widespread use of citizens' committees to support his candidacy. This technique was also used by Wendell Willkie in 1940. His backers had set up Willkie Clubs that built enough support to help him win the nomination, although he had no political experience. These citizens' clubs later worked for him during the election campaign.

The campaign of 1948, between Harry S. Truman and Thomas E. Dewey, is sometimes called the last of the whistle-stop campaigns, for in 1952 both candidates—Dwight D. Eisenhower and Adlai E. Stevenson—did most of their traveling by plane. This same election of 1952 marked the first major use of television as a channel for reaching the voters.

By 1960 television campaigning was no longer a novelty; in that year the big news was the four televised debates between John F. Kennedy and Richard M. Nixon. In the first debate, sixty million citizens who were spread across the country watched as the two presidential candidates met and argued face-to-face. Campaigning had come a long way since the early days of local political activity, limited voting, and silent candidates.

A Summing-up

Throughout our many different kinds of presidential campaigns, one point has remained unchanged. Each voter has always had to weigh those two big questions in his mind: Which candidate is best qualified to lead the country? How will I feel with him in the White House?

By Election Eve, each voter has probably answered those two questions to his own satisfaction. Now almost everyone is concentrating on a single thought: Who will win?

But if you read your newspapers carefully on this night before the election, you will find that a few men are asking other questions. In editorials and columns, in letters-to-the-editor, thoughtful people are analyzing the significance of our American way of electing a President. What are the advantages and strengths of our election system? What are its problems and weaknesses?

If you read these discussions, you will find yourself faced with these serious questions:

1. *Do we put too much emphasis on personalities during the campaign?* Do we study the issues carefully enough?

Are we too easily influenced by the public relations, advertising, TV and radio experts who help run campaigns? Can they really sell us a candidate's "image" with the same methods they use in commercials and advertisements that sell us soap? Are the candidates and parties to blame for enlisting these experts to help them sell candidates the same way soap is sold? Are we voters to blame because we do not educate ourselves on the facts of the issues?

Should the parties present more definite platforms? Should the candidates be responsible for presenting a thorough examination of the issues? Or is a candidate's personality more important than his party's platform?

2. *Why do so many citizens take no active part in the campaign?* Surveys show that only one out of every ten Americans is active enough politically to do more than vote. Although many millions read and talk and argue about the election, only one-tenth of the people go canvassing for votes, organize meetings, contribute money for candidates.

Is this because Americans still share the founding fathers' suspicion of political parties? Is it because we feel that our contribution of time or money would be unimportant? Is it because so many of us have been brought up to believe that politics is the business of professional politicians, not of all citizens? Would we have a stronger democracy if more citizens became active amateur politicians? Or is it enough for a citizen to decide and then vote?

3. *How good or poor* is *our record as voters?* Statistics show that no more than 64% of all Americans of voting age turn out at the polls in presidential elections.

What keeps the remaining 36% from the polls? We cannot say that all of the non-voters stay away from the polls because they do not want to vote. Experts estimate that roughly half of these non-voters are actually unable to vote because of state voting requirements, or because of conditions they cannot control.*

Do we need to change our state election laws to make voting easier? Should the states eliminate the literacy and residence requirements? Should they simplify the regulations for registration, and for voting by absentee ballot?

And what about the other half of the non-voters? Would it be a mistake to urge them to vote if they are disinterested and possibly not well-informed? Or should we look for new ways to get them to the polls?

* In every election, millions of citizens who have recently moved cannot meet state requirements regarding length of residence. Millions who cannot read and write are unable to meet state literacy requirements. Many hundreds of thousands are in prisons, homes for the aged or other institutions, and are not eligible to vote. Millions more are too ill to get to the polls on Election Day; and other millions have to be away from home on Election Day and have not applied in time for absentee ballots.

Then too, in some sections of the South, state election laws have been used to prevent or discourage millions of Negro citizens from voting. These laws were eliminated by the Voting Rights Act passed by Congress in 1965. But no one knows how much the 1968 turnout will be affected by this new law, and by the efforts of civil rights workers to increase Negro registration in the South.

How might they become more interested and better informed? What might be done by schools, newspapers and TV, campaign managers, parties, candidates, to increase our voting turnout?

4. *And what about paying for campaigns?* Although nobody knows the exact figures, everyone knows that presidential election campaigns cost a great deal. The whistle-stop trains and torchlight parades of old-time campaigns cost very little when compared with the jet planes, computers, public relations experts, and television broadcasts of today's campaigns. In 1964, almost $35,000,000 was spent by the Democratic and Republican national committees alone; and this was only a small part of the total spent in behalf of presidential candidates. Estimates of the total amount spent by national, state, local, and special interest groups in the 1964 campaign run as high as $200,000,000.

We also know that most of the money comes as large contributions from individuals and organizations giving strong support to the candidates whose election they believe will be best for them. But is this system best for the country? Are critics correct in saying that large contributions have too much influence on the candidates? Do we need a new approach? What should it be?

Should we have stronger laws to limit the size of contributions and the costs of campaigns? This would mean eliminating much of the high-speed plane travel and television broadcasting that bring the candidate and his ideas closer to so many millions of voters.

Or should we take the attitude that expensive campaigns are necessary under our democratic system—and that it's up to the government to pay for them? Might the government prohibit *all* political contributions and pay campaign costs out of the Treasury?

Or should all citizens be asked to contribute small sums to the candidate they favor? Should the government encourage this by allowing a citizen to take a tax deduction for making small political contributions? Would this promote broader participation in political campaigns? Or might people consider that they were being pressured to pay the costs of electioneering, and would they resent the pressure? Above all, could enough money be raised this way to make it practical for the government to prohibit or restrict large contributions?

Are there other practical methods for making larger contributions less important? In an attempt to answer this question, Congress passed a law in 1966 allowing every taxpayer to direct the Treasury to put $1 of his income tax payment into a special campaign fund for presidential elections. But the law was criticized for containing many loopholes, and it was repealed befor it could go into effect for the 1968 campaign. Congress is considering many other proposals con-

cerning campaign costs and how they are to be met
with many members of both parties hopeful that a
workable law can be passed before the next campaign.

These are the troubling questions you may read in
some papers, or hear discussed in quiet radio interviews, on the eve of the election. These questions are
important ones to remember, after the campaign excitement has died down; but at the time, few of us pay
attention to them.

Instead, we watch the eleventh-hour television programs produced by both parties. We read the last-
minute descriptions of each candidate's final public
appearance. We listen to the endless guesses of how
the voting will go. We are completely absorbed in wondering who is going to win when the voters go to the
polls tomorrow.

8

Act Four...
Election Day

In your town, the Tuesday after the first Monday in November may be warm and sunny, or gray and rainy, or cold and snowy.* Whatever the weather, Election Day throughout the land seems suddenly quiet.

The campaigning, the speechmaking, the arguing have stopped. Signs at the polls in every precinct declare, "No Electioneering at the Polls." Voting booths have been set up in schoolhouses and firehouses, in

---

* The weather is often said to affect the outcome of an election. Old-time political myths have it that fine weather means a large turnout of voters, including many independents and some others who are not usually particularly interested in politics. But rain or snow supposedly keeps many such people away from the polls; then the election is more likely to be decided by the party regulars who would fight their way through blizzards, if necessary, to cast their ballots. Sometimes in an area where the Republican party is stronger, bad weather will be called "Republican weather," on the assumption that the wavering independents and Democrats won't make it to the polls. And the reverse is true of sections that are Democratic strongholds.

town halls and empty stores; and all during the quiet day the people stand in line outside the polls.

Once inside, each voter must tell his name to an election clerk who checks the official list to be sure that the voter has registered. Then each man or woman walks into a small booth, closes the curtain, and casts a ballot.

After all the ballyhoo and booming, each citizen votes secretly in the curtained booth. Then each goes on to factory or office, or home to feed the chickens or take the baby for a walk. For most citizens, Election Day is a quiet day of waiting.

The Campaign Goes On

But for each party's precinct workers, the day is a busy one. Though the ballyhoo, speeches, and booming have stopped, the battle for votes continues and there are many political jobs to be done.

Some party members work as poll watchers; they spend the day at the polls as official representatives of their party. Each party appoints a watcher for every polling place; state laws require this. The poll watcher's job is to protect the party's interests: to double-check that only qualified citizens vote and that no qualified citizen is denied the right to vote; and to guarantee that the votes are later counted honestly and accurately.

Other precinct volunteers take on the job of making certain that the party's supporters turn out to vote. These volunteers station themselves at the polls.* They study the party's file cards showing which voters are "safe" for their candidate; and they check off these cards as the people arrive to vote. Later in the day they will call supporters who have not yet come to the polls.

By late afternoon, still more party workers go into action. Some organize car pools to bring voters to the polls. Others take on baby-sitting chores to give busy mothers time to cast their ballots. As we have seen, every vote counts; neither party wants to lose a single vote for its presidential candidate.

As dusk falls, a few late-comers hurry to the polls. By now tens of millions of people have cast their ballots, and soon the polls will close in each state and the vote-counting will begin.

The Returns Come In

As millions of families sit down to eat supper, they turn on radio and television sets. The election returns are beginning to come in, and the nation is eager to know how the balloting has gone.

The votes come in slowly at first. In the television

* These volunteers at the polls are working for their parties; but they are not official party representatives, chosen according to state election laws, as the poll watchers are.

studios, the election figures are listed by states on large scoreboards, but the votes are still too scattered to have much meaning or excitement. Newsmen fill in the time by reporting on the day's activities. Occasionally, the television cameras switch to the candidates' headquarters, where both campaign managers sound confident but, along with the rest of the country, anxiously watch the returns.

As more figures are posted, news commentators explain the significance of these early returns. State by state, they carefully watch certain sample areas that have been selected by election experts as typical voting districts—districts where the voting in past elections had followed the national pattern. The early results from these districts are fed into computers which are used to predict the probable outcome of this national election. In this prediction business, there is stiff competition among the TV networks, for each one wants the glory of being first with the correct prediction of who will win.

But in spite of computers and typical voting districts, people keep watching the actual voting figures roll up on the scoreboards, and listening to personal predictions from politicians and other experts who comment on—and even argue with—the computer results.

The predictions may change from hour to hour as the lead seesaws between the candidates. One man may be ahead in the Southern states while the other has a big lead in the Midwest or the East. The big-city vote may be going for Boyle while the rural vote favors Webber.

Every politician and commentator and citizen is watching for trends, studying the votes piling up in each section of the country and in each state. Boyle is running strong in New York . . . Webber is leading in Michigan . . . Pennsylvania is a tossup . . . Ohio is swinging to Webber . . . Boyle is moving ahead in Illinois . . . California is still a big question mark.*

You may hear a bewildering variety of predictions: "Webber will win by a landslide"—a tremendous majority of voters in his favor. Or: "It will be a squeak-in for Boyle"—a close race with both men running neck-and-neck until Boyle pulls ahead at the last minute.

Strangest of all, you may even hear this prediction: "Webber—or Boyle—may become President although he will not have the most votes!"

Can this really happen? Doesn't the majority always rule?

Yes, of course a majority rules. But in our American national elections, the President is elected by a majority of *electoral* votes, not popular votes.

---

* West-coast returns always come in later because the United States is divided into different time zones. Since Pacific Standard Time is three hours earlier than Eastern Standard Time, the polls in the Western states are still open when the Eastern states have already closed their polls and begun their vote-counting.

What Are Electoral Votes?

Popular votes are votes cast by the people—by the voters who go to the polls on Election Day.

Electoral votes are votes cast by the 50 states and the District of Columbia.* In each state, all the electoral votes will go to the presidential candidate who wins the most popular votes in that state. Some states have more electoral votes than others; this is why everyone is eager to know which candidate is ahead in certain states.

This is how our electoral system works:

Under the Constitution, each state casts as many electoral votes as it has Senators and Representatives in Congress. Each state, of course, has two Senators; but the number of Representatives is based on the state's population. States with more people have more Representatives—and thus more electoral votes— than states with fewer people. In every state, each party with a presidential candidate names people as electors to cast the state's electoral votes.

When a citizen votes in a presidential election, he is actually voting for Democratic or Republican or third party electors in his state; later these electors

* The Twenty-third Amendment to the Constitution, adopted in 1961, gave residents of the District of Columbia the right to vote for President, a right which they exercised for the first time in 1964. Thus, there are now 51 sets of electoral votes, totalling 538 votes: the 50 sets from the states, totalling 535, plus 3 electoral votes from the District of Columbia.

will vote for one of the presidential candidates. Many citizens do not realize this. In about half the states, the electors' names are not even printed on the ballots; only the candidates' names appear.

The electors do not really choose the President. In fact, the electors do not meet to vote until December, many weeks after the election results are known.

The state's electors who vote in December are the ones whose party's candidate has won the highest number of popular votes in their state. If the Democratic presidential candidate carries Wisconsin, Wisconsin's Democratic electors will gather to cast Wisconsin's electoral votes. If the Republican candidate wins in Pennsylvania, the men who cast Pennsylvania's electoral votes will be the Republican electors.

So when a state's electors meet, they are simply going through the formality of casting the state's electoral votes for their own party's presidential candidate.

A state's electoral votes cannot be divided between Democrats and Republicans. The party receiving the most popular votes in a state receives *all* of that state's electoral votes. The losing party in that state receives no electoral votes. It must be all or nothing in each state.

This is why the Election Night returns are carefully tallied state-by-state. As the popular votes are being counted, the country watches to see which candidate is leading in each state. In each state, remember, it will be a case of winner-takes-all—all the electoral votes.

Our new President will be the candidate who wins a majority of the electoral votes. This is stated clearly in the Constitution.

But what if no presidential candidate wins a majority? Suppose the electoral vote is a tie between the two candidates? Or suppose there are more than two candidates receiving electoral votes, and the top man gets a **plurality,** rather than a **majority,** of the votes?*

The Constitution has a clear answer for that, too. If there is no electoral-vote majority, the President is chosen by the House of Representatives. When the House votes, each state casts just one vote. The candidate who wins a majority of the states' votes becomes President. In our entire history, we've had just two elections—those of 1800 and 1824—that were thrown into the House.**

* An electoral-vote plurality would result if a third-party candidate won in a number of states, taking away enough electoral votes to prevent a majority from going to the Democrat or Republican who would have won in a two-party race.

It might also occur if enough Republican or Democratic electors should decide not to vote for their party's candidate. On a few occasions, an elector has been known to vote for someone other than his party's candidate; but because of the small number of electors involved, this has never affected the outcome of a presidential election. (To learn how and why it could be significant, see pages 131 and 132.)

** The election of 1800 produced a tie among the electors and went to the House of Representatives. The House could not produce a majority decision for 35 ballots. On the 36th ballot, Thomas Jeffer-

That Strange Prediction

The chart on page 120 shows how the country's 538 electoral votes are divided. New figures are worked out every ten years, when the government takes a census of the entire population. The figures shown in this chart are for the 1964 and the 1968 elections and are based on the 1960 census. The figures for the election of 1972 will probably be different since they will be based on the 1970 census.

If you will study the chart, you will understand the reason for the strange fact that a candidate may become President even though he may not have a majority of the popular votes. To win the election, a candidate must capture 270 of the 538 electoral votes. Notice that the seven states with the largest populations total 210 electoral votes among them: New York, California, Pennsylvania, Illinois, Ohio, Texas, Michigan.

If a candidate—Boyle for instance—could carry these seven states, he would be well on his way toward that electoral-vote majority. He might reach the

son was elected. (For more details on this very unusual election, see footnote 2 in the Presidential Elections chart on pages 151 and 152.)

The 1824 election, with four presidential candidates, resulted in an electoral-vote plurality. Andrew Jackson was top man with 99 votes; John Quincy Adams was runner-up with 84. (The remaining 78 votes were divided between the two other candidates.) But when the vote went to the House, 13 of the 24 states cast ballots for Adams, making him the President.

necessary 270 votes by carrying as few as five more of the states with large electoral votes.

How the Electoral Votes are Divided

Alabama	10	Nebraska	5
Alaska	3	Nevada	3
Arizona	5	New Hampshire	4
Arkansas	6	New Jersey	17
California	40	New Mexico	4
Colorado	6	New York	43
Connecticut	8	North Carolina	13
Delaware	3	North Dakota	4
Florida	14	Ohio	26
Georgia	12	Oklahoma	8
Hawaii	4	Oregon	6
Idaho	4	Pennsylvania	29
Illinois	26	Rhode Island	4
Indiana	13	South Carolina	8
Iowa	9	South Dakota	4
Kansas	7	Tennessee	11
Kentucky	9	Texas	25
Louisiana	10	Utah	4
Maine	4	Vermont	3
Maryland	10	Virginia	12
Massachusetts	14	Washington	9
Michigan	21	West Virginia	7
Minnesota	10	Wisconsin	12
Mississippi	7	Wyoming	3
Missouri	12	District of Columbia	3
Montana	4		

538

Now, imagine that Boyle does carry these twelve larger states, but that he wins each state by only a slim margin of popular votes. Imagine, too, that Webber carries all the other states by large popular majorities. Webber would lose the election, even though his total popular vote might be bigger than Boyle's.

This imaginary example is not a strong possibility. Usually the man who leads in popular votes does win an electoral-vote majority; but there is always that slim chance that the two sets of votes will not produce the same winner. And we actually have had three Presidents who won fewer popular votes than their major opponents.

The first time this happened was in 1824. In this four-way race, Andrew Jackson led in popular votes and John Quincy Adams was the runner-up. But Jackson failed to win a majority of electoral votes; he won only a plurality. The election, therefore, was thrown into the House of Representatives, which chose Adams for President.

In two later elections, the candidates who won electoral-vote majorities trailed behind their opponents in popular votes. In 1876, Rutherford B. Hayes became President although Samuel J. Tilden won more popular votes.* And in 1888 Benjamin

* This was a remarkable election for several reasons. The electoral votes were unbelievably close: 185 for Hayes, 184 for Tilden. What's more, before the final official tally, the electoral vote stood at 165

Harrison won the Presidency despite Grover Cleveland's lead in popular votes.

In both elections, the popular votes were very close. But in both cases that slim margin of popular votes was not enough; both popular-vote winners lost the election because they lost the electoral vote. And it is a majority of the electoral votes that decides our presidential elections.

States' Electoral Votes are All-important

Now you can see why the states are so important in our national elections, and why political parties are organized on a statewide basis. A party's strength in a presidential election depends on whether it can carry enough states to gain a majority of the electoral votes.

So while the popular votes are being counted on Election Night, everyone is eagerly watching to see which particular states each candidate will carry. The number of states a man carries is not all-important; neither is the total popular vote for each candidate.

The important question is: "How are the popular votes distributed?" Which man is leading in which

---

for Hayes and 184 for Tilden. The remaining 20 electoral votes, from four states, were undecided because the parties were arguing about the honesty of these states' election returns. Congress appointed an Electoral Commission to settle the arguments; the Commission, which had a majority of Republicans, gave all 20 disputed votes to Hayes, the Republican candidate.

states? And how do those states' electoral votes add up?

In the 1960 presidential election, for instance, John F. Kennedy won 34,227,096 popular votes to Richard M. Nixon's 34,108,546. That was a very narrow margin of victory. But Kennedy's popular votes were distributed in such a way that he won a fairly comfortable electoral-vote majority. He needed 269 electoral votes to win; he received 303. Kennedy carried only twenty-two states, but among these were five of the seven largest states. Although Nixon won in more than half the states, he did not carry enough large states.

Sometimes, however, it may be a smaller state that holds the key to victory in a close election. A handful of popular votes can swing an entire state into a candidate's column. And that single state may be the one to give the candidate an electoral-vote majority—and the Presidency.

That was precisely what happened in 1916, in the tight race between President Woodrow Wilson and Charles Evans Hughes. During the vote-counting, Hughes was leading in electoral votes all the way. He actually went to bed on Election Night thinking that he had won the Presidency; many newspapers published extras announcing his victory.

But the next morning it became obvious that California's vote was still in doubt. California, then one of the smaller states, had been considered safe for Hughes; he needed its few votes for his electoral-vote majority. As the late returns from California trickled in, the entire country was kept in suspense. At last, two days after the election, the complete returns showed that Wilson had carried California by exactly 3,773 votes. The state's few electoral votes—just thirteen—swung into Wilson's column and gave him the election.

Here again, the important question was how the popular vote was distributed. Less than 4,000 popular votes in the crucial state of California re-elected Woodrow Wilson.

As you examine our electoral system, you can understand why a candidate must study his strength in every state, and why he must try to reach every voter during the campaign. Each candidate is always aware that his next speech may convince a small group of voters who can swing a necessary state into his column.

The Last Word

And on Election Night everyone studies the returns to learn which states are lining up in each candidate's column. What's happening in New York, Pennsylvania, Illinois, California, Massachusetts, New Jersey? Who's leading in Florida, Wisconsin, Tennessee,

Louisiana, Texas, Michigan, Georgia? Everyone is wondering which candidate will be first to total 270 electoral votes.

The trends may develop slowly or quickly. They may be definite or confusing. Within a few hours everyone may know who is the winner; or the questions may drag on into the early-morning hours.

The last official words of the campaign are the loser's concession of defeat and the winner's acceptance of the great honor the people have bestowed on him. You may see the loser making his concession statement on television; and you may watch the jubilant crowds cheering the winner at his headquarters. But sometimes the race is so close that the concession comes after most of the country has given up and gone to bed. Your first knowledge of the big news might then be the banner headline streaming across the front page of your morning newspaper.

However the news breaks, the long campaign is finally over, and the world knows who will be President of the United States for the next four years. But probably very few people outside our own country are aware of the complex electoral-vote system we follow in electing an American President.

9

A Backward Glance...
at the Electoral College

Our system of electoral votes may seem like a complicated, and even unfair, way to elect our President. To understand the reason for it, we must go back to the summer of 1787, when the founding fathers were writing the Constitution.

Those men spent days trying to decide this one question: How should the President of the United States be chosen?

Remember that kings were the rulers throughout the world in those days. The American people did not want a king, nor did their leaders. The founders decided that the government would be headed by a President, and that the Presidency would change hands regularly.

They wanted the country's best leaders to be selected for the Presidency. But they could not imagine how all the people could possibly choose the best President from among the country's leaders.

To begin with, the American states were stretched along the Atlantic coast for well over a thousand miles from northern New England down to Georgia. This was a tremendous distance in those days of horse and carriage, when it took three days to travel the ninety miles from New York to Philadelphia. How could these scattered citizens learn anything about a presidential candidate who might live in a far-distant state? Wouldn't the people of each state tend to vote only for the candidates from their own state?

Then too, some of the founders did not quite trust the good judgment of the people. Democracy—the people's right to rule themselves—was such a new idea at that time; many people simply took it for granted that some were born to lead and others to follow. Could the common people be trusted with such an important decision as the choice of a single national leader? Did they have the education, the information, the good sense to make such a choice? Might it not be wiser for the President to be selected by a special group of the country's outstanding public men? By Congress, perhaps? Or by the Governors of the states?

For days this question was argued during the Constitutional Convention. Only a few men thought that the people should vote for the President; most opposed this idea. Finally the founders agreed on a compromise: each state would choose electors who would, in turn, vote for the President and the Vice President.

The groups of electors from all the states came to be called the Electoral College.

How Would the Electoral College Work?

The founding fathers reasoned that each state would select its own best local leaders as electors. The electors, they expected, would be men of education and wisdom. They would exercise their own good judgment; they could be trusted with the selection of a national leader.

It was left up to each state to decide how the electors would be chosen. Actually, most of the founding fathers did not expect that the people themselves would vote for electors. They assumed that the electors would be chosen by the state legislatures.

This was how they thought that the system would work:

The citizens who could vote—and not many could, because of the strict property qualifications—would elect their state legislators. Each state legislature would select the electors for its state. And the electors would then vote for a President. So the choice of a national leader would be very far removed from the common people.

For several reasons, the Electoral College did not work out as the founding fathers had planned.

How the Electoral College Has Changed

As we have seen, political parties soon were formed in the young country. By the third presidential election, in 1796, the parties had taken on the job of nominating presidential candidates. That was the first change: the electors were presented with party-supported candidates from whom to choose.

During the early 1800's two more changes developed. A few states were allowing the people to vote directly for electors. And some states were beginning to remove property qualifications for voting. The democratic idea of government *by* the people was gradually becoming an accepted part of the American system.

By 1828, in all but two of the twenty-four states, the electors were chosen by popular elections, not by state legislatures. And almost all male citizens, not just property owners, had the right to vote in these elections.

The basic purpose of the Electoral College had changed. It now worked this way:

Each party in a state named electors who would vote for its presidential candidate. A citizen knew, when he voted for a party's electors, that these men would vote for the party's candidate. The electors did not exercise their own judgment. The electors of the winning party almost automatically cast the state's electoral votes for their party's candidate—the candidate who had been chosen by the people in the state.

This was how the choice of a national leader came much closer to the common people than the founding fathers had intended it to. Within forty years of the Constitution's ratification, the people had won the power to elect their President. And this is how the Electoral College still works today.*

Are Other Changes Coming?

Some experts argue that the method of electing a President can be improved. They say the present Electoral College is weak because:

—There is always the possibility that the popular-vote winner in a close election might lose the election because he has won those popular votes in states that do not give him enough electoral votes. This has happened three times.

—It is legally possible for some electors to vote against their party's candidate. When electors are chosen by a state party, it is assumed that they will vote for the party's candidate. But not all state laws require electors to pledge themselves to do this. In

* Though called a "college," the groups of state electors never meet as a united body. All the electors vote on the same day in December; but each state's winning electors gather in their own state, usually in the capital. The votes of all the states' electors are sent to Washington where they are opened, early in January, at a joint session of Congress.

fact, several states' laws specifically say that electors *must* be allowed to remain unpledged. So we might have the situation where one party earned enough electoral votes to give the election to its candidate— but if enough unpledged electors refused to vote for him, the candidate might be denied an electoral-vote majority. This would throw the election into the House of Representatives.

—Then too, we might have a situation where a third-party candidate had won in some states and had thus received enough electoral votes to prevent either major-party candidate from having an electoral-vote majority. If enough of the third-party candidate's electors were unpledged, he could, in effect, decide who was going to be President by requesting those electors to vote for whichever major party candidate he named.

—Since all of a state's electoral votes go to the party of the candidate with the greatest number of popular votes, the votes of the people who cast their ballots for the losing party in that state count for nothing.

—The present system gives too much weight to each popular vote in the states with the smallest population. For instance, California has 40 electoral votes to Alaska's 3—about thirteen times as many. But California's population is about sixty-five times as great as the population of Alaska. So each citizen's ballot cast in Alaska actually has five times the weight of a ballot cast in California.

—The popular vote has even less meaning if the vote is thrown into the House of Representatives for lack of an electoral vote majority. In the House, each state casts only one vote and a majority is needed. This means that states with large populations have no more say about the choice of a President than do those with small populations. It also means that the 450,000 people in Nevada, for instance, have as big a voice in the House's decision as the 18,000,000 people in New York. Putting it another way, it would be possible for the President to be selected by the representatives of the people in the twenty-six smallest states—states with populations totalling 34,000,000, in a country with an overall population of more than 200,000,000.

For many years, various suggestions have been made for correcting these weaknesses in the Electoral College. Some that are being seriously considered at present are:

—to abolish the Electoral College and let citizens vote directly for the President, who could be elected by a 40 per cent plurality of the popular vote;

—to abolish the Electoral College, but keep the states' electoral votes, with each state's entire electoral vote going automatically to the candidate who carries that state;

—to abolish the Electoral College, but keep the states' electoral votes, with each state's electoral vote being divided among the candidates so that each man would receive electoral votes in the same proportion as the percentage of popular votes he won in the state;

—to keep the Electoral College, but allow an electoral plurality of 40 per cent, instead of a majority, to elect a President, thus making it much less likely that any election would be thrown into the House of Representatives.

Any one of these plans would require a Constitutional amendment; and a number of amendments based on these suggestions have been introduced into Congress during the past few years. Because new problems require new ideas and new solutions, our Constitution was planned to allow for changes. But ratification of a Constitutional amendment is usually a slow and difficult process, and it is not likely that any Electoral College amendment will be passed in time to affect the 1968 presidential election.

A Summing-up

The changing role of the Electoral College is only one example of how our presidential elections have kept pace with the growth of democracy. The United States has seen forty-six presidential election years between 1789 and 1968. And each one has had its own surprises, new ideas, new developments.

Think back over the changes that have occurred:

Two powerful political parties direct our campaigns—though the founding fathers didn't want parties at all.

Party members vote in primary elections and at state conventions to show their preferences for candidates—though early leaders didn't dream of consulting the common people on such an important question.

Thousands of politicians meet at huge national conventions to nominate presidential candidates—though candidates were first chosen at small, secret Congressional caucuses.

The candidates stump the nation, meeting voters everywhere—though nineteenth-century Americans would have been shocked by this undignified behavior.

On Election Day, every registered citizen has the right to vote—though the original thirteen states reserved this right for property owners.

The Electoral College is considered, for the most part, just an echo of the voice of the people—though the founding fathers planned that the electors would be special men, privileged to make a decision that the common people couldn't be trusted with.

America's founders wrote a basic law that allowed democracy to grow. They knew that a government of free men must be a changing government; and they gave us a Constitution that provides lawful, peaceable ways to bring about those changes.

10

Epilogue...
The New President
Takes Over

It is January of a new year—the year after the presidential campaign, the year that begins a new presidential administration.

Inauguration Day is January 20. In Washington this is a day of celebration, of parades, of parties and presidential balls. The capital is crowded with visitors invited to take part in the celebration. For the winning party, this is a great day: thousands of its politicians and campaign workers gather here from every state.

But the President is the newly elected head of the entire country, not just the leader of a party. Democrats and Republicans alike watch the inaugural ceremony on television or read the details in their newspapers; this is a day that touches the whole nation.

The day's highlight is the solemn, hushed moment at noon when the new President takes the oath of office. The ceremony is held outdoors in front of the Capitol, the building where Congress meets. The weather may be icy and biting, but huge crowds turn out to watch as the Chief Justice of the United States administers the oath.

After the President has been sworn in, he makes his Inaugural Address. Speaking to all the citizens, he tells of his hopes, and perhaps his fears, for the coming four years. He sums up for his countrymen the goals he has set for his new administration.

Then he drives down broad Constitution Avenue and Pennsylvania Avenue to the White House, leading a parade of thousands. There are military bands and drum majorettes and beauty queens, midshipmen from Annapolis, cadets from West Point, Texas cowboys on bucking broncos, citizens representing every part of the United States.

Today's inauguration is a very different scene from the country's first inauguration. George Washington sat in a cream-colored coach drawn by four horses. The soldiers in his parade were brilliantly uniformed dragoons and grenadiers. Their line of march was through the narrow streets of old New York, then the nation's capital.

When Washington stood on the balcony of New York's Federal Hall, he set the inauguration pattern that has been followed by every American President. Washington placed his hand on the Bible, repeated the presidential oath, then said, "I swear, so help me God."

With this same oath, each of our Presidents has taken office:

I do solemnly swear (or affirm) that I will faithfully execute the office of the President of the United States and will, to the best of my ability, preserve, protect, and defend the Constitution of the United States.

Thus each President begins his term. At this moment of oath-taking the noise and turbulence of the election year are far from most Americans' minds. Now the campaign is in the past.

This is the beginning of a new year, a new administration. There are old and new problems for the country to face under the guidance of its newly elected leader.

Glossary

ballot. A paper bearing the names of the candidates in an election. The voter may mark his choice with a pencil or, if voting machines are used, he will pull a lever that automatically marks his vote on one ballot. The ballot took its name from **balla,** the Italian word for "ball"; long ago each voter was given a small ball which he placed in a box bearing the name of the candidate he chose.

bandwagon. A political campaign that seems almost certain of being successful. **To jump on the bandwagon** means to side with the candidate who appears most likely to win. The expression comes from the old-time campaign custom of staging colorful parades for political candidates; a parade would be led by a brass band riding on a large wagon. If a local politician was certain that the particular candidate was a sure winner, he would jump aboard the musicians' bandwagon to show the townspeople that he was supporting the candidate.

bloc. See **pressure group.**

Cabinet. A group of advisors whom the President appoints to assist him. The Cabinet members, who meet regularly with the President, are the heads of the twelve government departments: State; Treasury; Defense; Justice; Post Office; Interior; Agriculture; Commerce; Labor; Health, Education and Welfare; Housing and Urban Development; and Transportation.

candidate. A person chosen by a political party to seek a public office.

caucus. A meeting of party leaders to decide on candidates or other party business. This odd word (pronounced KAW-kuhs) is an American invention. Scholars are unsure of how it originated but most think that it comes from the Algonquin Indian word *caucauasu* meaning: "one who advises, urges, or encourages."

Congress. The legislature of the United States government. Congress consists of two separate sections, called houses: the Senate and the House of Representatives.

Congressman. See **Representative.**

dark horse. A presidential hopeful who is not well-known and seems to have little chance of winning a nomination. At one time in England jockeys might plot to win races by entering a famous fast horse, but disguising him by dyeing his hair and coat. Usually black dye was used. When the "dark horse" won, everyone would be astonished because they had assumed he was an unknown racer.

draft. To nominate a candidate through pressure from the party or from large masses of the voters. In theory, at least, a draft movement means that the party has sought out the candidate; supposedly the man does not actively work for the nomination.

Governor. The person elected to head the government of a state, in the United States. The Governor's job is to enforce the state's laws.

grassroots. Close to the average voter. A grassroots campaign is one which enlists the help of many citizen volunteers. Originally the word indicated that the volunteer aid sprang up spontaneously in country areas, far from the big political organizations in the cities.

inauguration. The ceremony that takes place when the President is sworn into office.

independent voter. A voter who does not belong to any political party.

legislature. The branch of the government that makes the laws. Members of a state legislature are elected by voters in the state and make laws for the people of that state.

majority. At least one more than half of the total.

National Committee. Two representatives—one man and one woman—from each state and territory; they are chosen at the nominating convention, and make all necessary plans for the following nominating convention. Committee members are usually active in their own state organizations between and during presidential campaigns.

nominate. To name a candidate.

party member. A voter who is enrolled, according to state election laws, with a political party. Citizens may enroll as party members when they register to vote. See **register.**

plank. One section of a party's campaign platform. Each plank in the platform is devoted to a particular issue.

platform. A party's statement of its policies on important public issues.

plurality. The number of votes by which the top man leads the runner-up in an election race among three or more candidates. For a simple example of a plurality vote, imagine that three candidates are competing for 100 votes. The final vote is: A—45; B—35; C—20. A is the top man, with more votes than anyone else; but he does not have a majority, which would be 51. Since A leads runner-up B by 10 votes, A has a plurality of 10 in the election race.

political party.   An organization of voters working to gain control of the government by nominating and electing its candidates for public office.

politician.   A professional politician is a person whose job is concerned with political affairs. He may be an elected official, or he may be employed by a political party. See **politics.**

politics.   The practical art of gaining governmental power by winning elections, and of keeping power through successful policies between elections.

poll.   See **public-opinion survey.**

polls.   The place where voters cast their ballots in an election.

poll-taker.   An interviewer for a public-opinion survey, or poll.

precinct.   The smallest voting district. Each precinct has definite boundaries; everyone living within those boundaries votes at one polling place. There are about 150,000 precincts in the United States; an average of 500 to 600 voters may live in each one.

presidential primary election (also called **presidential preferential primary**).   A "nominating" election which allows voters who belong to a political party to show which man they prefer as the party's candidate for President. In most states, a presidential primary is a "closed primary": a voter must be an enrolled party member in order to vote in that party's primary. Some states have experimented with the "open primary" in which any voter may cast a ballot to show which man he prefers as the party's candidate; this kind of primary is open to independent voters and even to members of other political parties. Only a few states still use open primaries.

pressure group. An organization of citizens who share a common interest and work actively to achieve certain goals. In some ways a pressure group resembles a political party because it favors certain public policies and tries to have laws passed that will promote these policies. But it uses different methods from those used by parties. Instead of nominating candidates for public office and seeking control of the government, a pressure group tries to influence the political parties. During election campaigns, it often supports party candidates who agree with its policies. At other times, it tries to build public support for its policies and to urge the parties to pass laws that will benefit its members. A large pressure group, or a combination of co-operating groups, often claims to represent an influential *bloc* of voters—many citizens who think alike and supposedly will vote alike. The various farmers' organizations, for instance, are said to represent the farm bloc.

public-opinion survey. A method of learning what people think about important public questions. The survey is conducted by an organization that sends interviewers to ask questions of a small group of people; these people are considered typical of the entire population, or of certain groups within the population. A survey is also called a public-opinion *poll*.

register as a party member. To record a voter's name, with state election officials, as a member of one particular political party. Any citizen who is eligible to vote may—if he wishes—sign up as a member of a political party. Party registration allows a citizen to vote in any primary election his party may hold to select candidates.

register as a voter. To record a voter's name on the state's official list of those entitled to vote. In every state, a citizen must register with local election officials in order to vote. In some states, registration must be repeated at a certain time before each election. Other states use permanent registration systems: after a voter registers once, his name is kept on the official list, although he must notify election officials if he moves. In every state a citizen must meet certain qualifications before he can register. He must be a certain age, for instance, and he must have lived in the state for a certain length of time. Another common requirement is evidence of literacy, the ability to read and write.

Representative.   A member of the House of Representatives, the larger house of the United States Congress. There are 435 Representatives in the House; the number of Representatives elected by each state is based on the state's population. Representatives are often called **Congressmen.**

Senator.   A member of the Senate, the smaller house of the United States Congress. Since each state elects two Senators, there is a total of 100 Senators. The Senate is sometimes called the "upper house" of Congress.

take the stump.   Make campaign speeches. This phrase originated in the early days of American politics when a local candidate campaigning on the frontier would often speak at an outdoor meeting and use a tree stump as a speaker's platform.

third party.   In the United States, any political party other than the two major national parties. A third party is sometimes organized by "bolters" from a major party who are dissatisfied with the major party's position on one or more important issues. Or a third party may be organized by independents in a particular area to promote an issue that is popular with the people of that section. Many third parties are organized in just one state to run local, state, or Congressional candidates. Other third parties do run presidential candidates, but they seldom place these candidates on the ballots in every state. It is difficult for a third party to build a strong working organization in every state and to conduct a well-organized coast-to-coast campaign.

toss his hat into the ring. To announce that one is willing to be his party's candidate for a public office, especially for the presidential nomination. It was an old frontier custom for a man to throw his hat, coat, or shirt into the boxing ring to show that he was volunteering to wrestle or fight an opponent. This phrase was first used in a political sense by ex-President Theodore Roosevelt. Early in 1912 many people were urging Roosevelt to run again for the Presidency. When a reporter asked whether he would be a candidate, Roosevelt answered, "My hat is in the ring."

Election Year	President and Party	Major Opponent and Party
1789	George Washington[1] *No party*	John Adams[1] *No party*
1792	George Washington[1] *No party*	John Adams[1] *No party*
1796	John Adams[1] *Federalist*	Thomas Jefferson[1] *Democratic-Republican*
1800	Thomas Jefferson[1, 2] *Democratic-Republican*	Aaron Burr[1, 2] *Democratic-Republican*
1804	Thomas Jefferson *Democratic-Republican*	Charles C. Pinckney *Federalist*
1808	James Madison *Democratic-Republican*	Charles C. Pinckney *Federalist*
1812	James Madison *Democratic-Republican*	DeWitt Clinton *Federalist*
1816	James Monroe *Democratic-Republican*	Rufus King *Federalist*
1820	James Monroe *Democratic-Republican*	John Quincy Adams *National-Republican*
1824	John Quincy Adams *National-Republican*	Andrew Jackson *Democratic-Republican*
1828	Andrew Jackson *Democrat*	John Quincy Adams *National-Republican*
1832	Andrew Jackson *Democrat*	Henry Clay *National-Republican*
1836	Martin Van Buren *Democrat*	William H. Harrison *Whig*
1840	William H. Harrison *Whig* (John Tyler)[5]	Martin Van Buren *Democrat*
1844	James K. Polk *Democrat*	Henry Clay *Whig*
1848	Zachary Taylor *Whig* (Millard Fillmore)[6]	Lewis Cass *Democrat*

IN THE UNITED STATES

| Electoral Votes | | Total |
Winner	Loser	Electoral Votes
69	34	See Footnote 1
132	77	See Footnote 1
71	68	See Footnote 1
73[2]	73[2]	See Footnote 1
162	14	176
122	47	175[3]
128	89	217
183	34	217
231	1	232
84[4]	99	261
178	83	261
219	49	286
170	73	294
234	60	294
170	105	275
163	127	290

1852	Franklin Pierce *Democrat*	Winfield Scott *Whig*
1856	James Buchanan *Democrat*	John C. Fremont *Republican*
1860	Abraham Lincoln *Republican*	John C. Breckinridge[7] *Democrat*
1864	Abraham Lincoln *Republican* (Andrew Johnson)[8]	George B. McClellan *Democrat*
1868	Ulysses S. Grant *Republican*	Horatio Seymour *Democrat*
1872	Ulysses S. Grant *Republican*	Horace Greeley *Liberal-Republican,* *Democrat*
1876	Rutherford B. Hayes *Republican*	Samuel J. Tilden *Democrat*
1880	James A. Garfield *Republican* (Chester A. Arthur)[10]	Winfield S. Hancock *Democrat*
1884	Grover Cleveland *Democrat*	James G. Blaine *Republican*
1888	Benjamin Harrison *Republican*	Grover Cleveland *Democrat*
1892	Grover Cleveland *Democrat*	Benjamin Harrison *Republican*
1896	William McKinley *Republican*	William J. Bryan *Democrat*
1900	William McKinley *Republican* (Theodore Roosevelt)[11]	William J. Bryan *Democrat*
1904	Theodore Roosevelt *Republican*	Alton B. Parker *Democrat*
1908	William H. Taft *Republican*	William J. Bryan *Democrat*
1912	Woodrow Wilson *Democrat*	Theodore Roosevelt *Progressive*
1916	Woodrow Wilson *Democrat*	Charles E. Hughes *Republican*

254	42	296
174	114	296
180	72	303
212	21	233
214	80	294
286	—[9]	349
185	184	369
214	155	369
219	182	401
233	168	401
277	145	444
271	176	447
292	155	447
336	140	476
321	162	483
435	88	531
277	254	531

1920	Warren G. Harding *Republican* (Calvin Coolidge)[12]	James M. Cox *Democrat*
1924	Calvin Coolidge *Republican*	John W. Davis *Democrat*
1928	Herbert Hoover *Republican*	Alfred E. Smith *Democrat*
1932	Franklin D. Roosevelt *Democrat*	Herbert Hoover *Republican*
1936	Franklin D. Roosevelt *Democrat*	Alfred Landon *Republican*
1940	Franklin D. Roosevelt *Democrat*	Wendell Willkie *Republican*
1944	Franklin D. Roosevelt *Democrat* (Harry S Truman)[13]	Thomas E. Dewey *Republican*
1948	Harry S Truman *Democrat*	Thomas E. Dewey *Republican*
1952	Dwight D. Eisenhower *Republican*	Adlai E. Stevenson *Democrat*
1956	Dwight D. Eisenhower *Republican*	Adlai E. Stevenson *Democrat*
1960	John F. Kennedy *Democrat* (Lyndon B. Johnson)[14]	Richard M. Nixon *Republican*
1964	Lyndon B. Johnson *Democrat*	Barry M. Goldwater *Republican*

1. In the first four presidential elections, electoral votes were cast according to the original Constitutional plan: each elector cast two votes, *on the same ballot,* for President and Vice President. The elector did not specify which candidate he wanted for President and which for Vice President. The candidate receiving the *highest number* of electoral votes became President, and the one receiving the second highest number became Vice President.

Thus in 1789, when George Washington received sixty-nine votes, with sixty-nine electors voting, he was the electors' unanimous choice for President; and in 1792 he was again elected unanimously, receiving one vote from each of the 132 electors.

John Adams, shown in the chart as George Washington's major opponent in 1789 and again in 1792, was actually the electors' second

404	127	531
382	136	531
444	87	531
472	59	531
523	8	531
449	82	531
432	99	531
303	189	531
442	89	531
457	73	531
303	219	537
486	52	538

choice as President in both elections; he therefore became Vice President both times.

2. By the end of Washington's second term, a national two-party system was developing. The elections of 1796 and 1800 showed that the original Constitutional plan for electoral voting would not work once this two-party system had become established.

In 1796, John Adams was elected President by a narrow majority of electoral votes; and Thomas Jefferson, his major opponent and the leader of the opposing political party, was elected to serve as Adams' Vice President.

Then, in 1800, Democratic-Republican Thomas Jefferson and his vice-presidential running mate, Aaron Burr, tied with 73 electoral votes. Their Federalist opponents were out of the running. (The

Federalist candidates were John Adams for President, and Charles C. Pinckney for Vice President.) Thus, when the election was thrown into the House of Representatives, Jefferson and Burr, who had run as a Democratic-Republican team, were pitted against each other for the Presidency. But the Federalists who controlled the House would not readily elect *any* Democratic-Republican President, and, for 35 ballots, Jefferson could not get a majority. On the 36th ballot, he won.

After the election, the Constitution was amended. Under the Twelfth Amendment, electors vote for President and Vice President on separate ballots. The winning presidential candidate must receive a majority of all the electoral votes cast for President; if no presidential candidate receives a majority, the vote goes to the House.

3. Note that in this election, and in many others later, the winner's electoral votes and the loser's electoral votes add up to less than the total electoral votes. In such elections, there were one or more other presidential candidates who received the remaining electoral votes.

4. No candidate received a majority of electoral votes in this four-way race. The House of Representatives chose John Quincy Adams as President.

5. President Harrison died one month after his inauguration, and Vice President John Tyler succeeded to the Presidency.

6. President Taylor died in 1850, and Vice President Millard Fillmore succeeded to the Presidency.

7. In 1860, there were four presidential candidates: Abraham Lincoln, Stephen A. Douglas, John C. Breckinridge, and John Bell. Douglas was considered Lincoln's major opponent in the election, and he came in second in popular votes. But Douglas came in fourth in electoral votes, receiving only 12. Breckinridge, who came in third in popular votes, received the second highest number of electoral votes.

8. President Lincoln was assassinated in 1865, and Vice President Andrew Johnson succeeded to the Presidency.

9. Greeley died three weeks after the election, before the Electoral College met; electoral votes cast for him were not counted.

10. President Garfield was assassinated in 1881, and Vice President Chester A. Arthur succeeded to the Presidency.

11. President McKinley was assassinated in 1901, and Vice President Theodore Roosevelt succeeded to the Presidency.

12. President Harding died in 1923, and Vice President Calvin Coolidge succeeded to the Presidency.

13. President Roosevelt died in 1945, and Vice President Harry S Truman succeeded to the Presidency.

14. President Kennedy was assassinated in 1963, and Vice President Lyndon B. Johnson succeeded to the Presidency.

Books About
Politics and the Presidency

Young People's Books

The Presidency, Gerald W. Johnson (Morrow, New York, 1962). Clear, brief explanation of what the President does, how the Presidency has changed, and which Presidents have done the most to effect these changes.

Diary of Democracy, Harry E. Neal (Messner, New York, 1962). A political history of America, from 1620 to the present, describing the development of minority parties as well as major ones.

Our Independence and the Constitution, Dorothy Canfield Fisher (Random House, Landmark Books, New York, 1950). Historical novel—from the Revolutionary War to the summer of 1787 when the founding fathers drafted the Constitution.

Politicians and What They Do, David Botter (Franklin Watts, New York, 1960). A journalist reports the daily routine of some contemporary politicians, from county leaders and state legislators to Congressmen, Senators, and Presidents.

America and Its Presidents, Earl Schenck Miers (Grosset &
   Dunlap, New York, 1964). An individual chapter on each
   President tells of the man, his life, and his administration.
The Great Constitution, Henry Steele Commager (Bobbs-
   Merrill, Indianapolis and New York, 1961). An outstanding historian's colorful, simple account of how our Constitution was hammered out by the founding fathers.
What Do You Think?, Alvin Schwartz (Dutton, New York,
   1966). How we all form opinions, and how and why poll-
   takers study public opinion. Includes material on elections,
   politics, propaganda, government, pressure groups.

General Books

Report of the County Chairman, James A. Michener (Random House, New York, 1961). A famous novelist describes
   his activities as the county chairman of a citizens' committee organized to work in the 1960 presidential campaign.
The Presidency, Stefan Lorant (Macmillan, New York, 1951).
   Pictorial history of presidential election campaigns, from
   1789 to 1948. Contains hundreds of sketches, political
   cartoons, and photographs.
The Crescent Dictionary of American Politics, Eugene J.
   McCarthy (Macmillan, New York, 1962). A handy ref-
   erence volume, written by a United States Senator, that
   defines more than one thousand terms relating to government, politics, and parties.
The Presidency (*American Heritage,* New York; special issue,
   August 1964). Well-illustrated articles, by experts, on both
   serious and light-hearted topics: campaigning; First Families; Vice-Presidents; how Presidents have handled the job.
Our Country's Presidents, Frank Freidel (National Geo-

graphic Society, Washington, D.C., 1966). A biography of each President and the highlights of each administration. Many handsome photographs, maps, paintings, old prints.

Advanced Reading

The Making of the President 1960, Theodore H. White (Atheneum, New York, 1961). Analyzes the 1960 presidential campaign, reporting the activities of the seven leading contenders who tossed their hats in the ring.

The Making of the President 1964, Theodore H. White (Atheneum, New York, 1965). The 1964 election: Goldwater's capture of the Republican nomination; both candidates' campaigns; the significance of the civil rights movement.

The Road to the White House, by the staff of the *New York Times* (McGraw-Hill, New York, 1965). Presents varied points of view as *Times* staff members describe and analyze the 1964 campaign, quoting often from news articles and columns.

Miracle at Philadelphia, Catherine Drinker Bowen (Little-Brown, Boston, 1966). Informal, well-written account of the Constitutional Convention, with emphasis on the delegates as individuals—their conflicting philosophies, arguments, compromises.

The American Presidency, Clinton Rossiter (Harcourt, Brace, Harvest Books, New York, 1960). A study of the Presidency's powers and limits, in the past and today.

The Dynamics of the American Presidency, edited by Donald Johnson and Jack Walker (Wiley, New York, 1964). Anthology of scholarly articles by political scientists, politicians, and journalists.

Selections from

The Constitution
of the United States

The following selections from the Constitution include the Preamble and articles dealing with voting and with the Presidency.

WE THE PEOPLE of the United States, in Order to form a more perfect Union, establish Justice, insure domestic Tranquility, provide for the common defence, promote the general Welfare, and secure the Blessings of Liberty to ourselves and our Posterity, do ordain and establish this Constitution for the United States of America.

Article II

SECTION 1.   The executive Power shall be vested in a President of the United States of America. He shall hold his Office during the Term of four Years, and, together with the Vice President, chosen for the same Term, be elected as follows

Each State shall appoint, in such Manner as the Legislature thereof may direct, a Number of Electors, equal to the whole

Number of Senators and Representatives to which the State may be entitled in the Congress: but no Senator or Representative, or Person holding an Office of Trust or Profit under the United States, shall be appointed an Elector.

[The Electors shall meet in their respective States, and vote by Ballot for two Persons, of whom one at least shall not be an Inhabitant of the same State with themselves. And they shall make a List of all the Persons voted for, and of the Number of Votes for each; which List they shall sign and certify, and transmit sealed to the Seat of the Government of the United States, directed to the President of the Senate. The President of the Senate shall, in the Presence of the Senate and House of Representatives, open all the Certificates, and the Votes shall then be counted. The Person having the greatest Number of Votes shall be the President, if such Number be a Majority of the whole Number of Electors appointed; and if there be more than one who have such Majority, and have an equal Number of Votes, then the House of Representatives shall immediately chuse by Ballot one of them for President; and if no Person have a Majority, then from the five highest on the List the said House shall in like Manner chuse the President. But in chusing the President, the Votes shall be taken by States, the Representation from each State having one Vote; A quorum for this Purpose shall consist of a Member or Members from two thirds of the States, and a Majority of all the States shall be necessary to a Choice. In every Case, after the Choice of the President, the Person having the greatest Number of Votes of the Electors shall be the Vice President. But if there should remain two or more who have equal Votes, the Senate shall chuse from them by Ballot the Vice President.]*

* This paragraph has been superseded by the Twelfth Amendment.

The Congress may determine the Time of chusing the Electors, and the Day on which they shall give their Votes; which
Day shall be the same throughout the United States.

No Person except a natural born Citizen, or a Citizen of
the United States, at the time of the Adoption of this Constitution, shall be eligible to the Office of President; neither shall
any Person be eligible to that Office who shall not have at-
tained to the Age of thirty five Years, and been fourteen
Years a Resident within the United States.

[In Case of the Removal of the President from Office, or of
his Death, Resignation, or Inability to discharge the Powers
and Duties of the said Office, the Same shall devolve on the
Vice President, and the Congress may by Law provide for the
Case of Removal, Death, Resignation or Inability, both of the
President and Vice President, declaring what Officer shall then
act as President, and such Officer shall act accordingly, until
the Disability be removed, or a President shall be elected.]*

The President shall, at stated Times, receive for his Services,
a Compensation, which shall neither be encreased nor dimin-
ished during the Period for which he shall have been elected,
and he shall not receive within that Period any other Emolu-
ment from the United States, or any of them.

Before he enter on the Execution of his Office, he shall take
the following Oath or Affirmation:—"I do solemnly swear
(or affirm) that I will faithfully execute the Office of President
of the United States, and will to the best of my Ability, preserve, protect and defend the Constitution of the United
States."

SECTION 2.   The President shall be Commander in Chief
of the Army and Navy of the United States, and of the Militia
of the several States, when called into the actual Service of the
United States; he may require the Opinion, in writing, of the
principal Officer in each of the executive Departments, upon

* This paragraph has been modified by the Twenty-fifth Amendment.

any Subject relating to the Duties of their respective Offices, and he shall have Power to grant Reprieves and Pardons for Offences against the United States, except in Cases of Impeachment.

He shall have Power, by and with the Advice and Consent of the Senate, to make Treaties, provided two thirds of the Senators present concur; and he shall nominate, and by and with the Advice and Consent of the Senate, shall appoint Ambassadors, other public Ministers and Consuls, Judges of the supreme Court, and all other Officers of the United States, whose Appointments are not herein otherwise provided for, and which shall be established by Law: but the Congress may by Law vest the Appointment of such inferior Officers, as they think proper, in the President alone, in the Courts of Law, or in the Heads of Departments.

The President shall have Power to fill up all Vacancies that may happen during the Recess of the Senate, by granting Commissions which shall expire at the End of their next Session.

SECTION 3. He shall from time to time give to the Congress Information of the State of the Union, and recommend to their Consideration such Measures as he shall judge necessary and expedient; he may, on extraordinary Occasions, convene both Houses, or either of them, and in case of Disagreement between them, with Respect to the Time of Adjournment, he may adjourn them to such Time as he shall think proper; he shall receive Ambassadors and other public Ministers; he shall take Care that the Laws be faithfully executed, and shall Commission all the Officers of the United States.

SECTION 4. The President, Vice President and all civil Officers of the United States, shall be removed from Office on Impeachment for, and Conviction of, Treason, Bribery, or other high Crimes and Misdemeanors.

Twelfth Amendment

(Ratified in 1804)

    The electors shall meet in their respective states and vote by ballot for President and Vice-President, one of whom, at least, shall not be an inhabitant of the same state with themselves; they shall name in their ballots the person voted for as President, and in distinct ballots the person voted for as Vice-President, and they shall make distinct lists of all persons voted for as President, and of all persons voted for as Vice-President, and of the number of votes for each, which lists they shall sign and certify, and transmit sealed to the seat of the government of the United States, directed to the President of the Senate;—The President of the Senate shall, in presence of the Senate and House of Representatives, open all the certificates and the votes shall then be counted;—The person having the greatest number of votes for President, shall be the President, if such number be a majority of the whole number of Electors appointed; and if no person have such majority, then from the persons having the highest numbers not exceeding three on the list of those voted for as President, the House of Representatives shall choose immediately, by ballot, the President. But in choosing the President, the votes shall be taken by states, the representation from each state having one vote; a quorum for this purpose shall consist of a member or members from two-thirds of the states, and a majority of all the states shall be necessary to a choice. [And if the House of Representatives shall not choose a President whenever the right of choice shall devolve upon them, before the fourth day of March next following, then the Vice-President shall act as President, as in the case of the death or other constitutional disability of the President.]* The person having the greatest number of votes as Vice-President, shall be the Vice-President, if such number be a majority of the whole number of Electors appointed, and if no person have a majority, then from the two highest numbers on the list, the Senate shall choose the Vice-President; a quorum for the purpose shall consist of two-thirds of the whole number of Senators, and a majority of the whole number shall be necessary to a choice. But no person constitutionally ineligible to the office of President shall be eligible to that of Vice-President of the United States.

Fourteenth Amendment

(Ratified in 1868)

SECTION 1.   All persons born or naturalized in the United States, and subject to the jurisdiction thereof, are citizens of the United States and of the State wherein they reside. No State shall make or enforce any law which shall abridge the privileges or immunities of citizens of the United States; nor shall any State deprive any person of life, liberty, or property, without due process of law; nor deny to any person within its jurisdiction the equal protection of the laws.

SECTION 2.   Representatives shall be apportioned among the several States according to their respective numbers, counting the whole number of persons in each State, excluding Indians not taxed. But when the right to vote at any

---

* This sentence has been superseded by SECTION 3 of the Twentieth Amendment.

election for the choice of electors for President and Vice President of the United States, Representatives in Congress, the Executive and Judicial officers of a State, or the members of the Legislature thereof, is denied to any of the male inhabitants of such State, being twenty-one years of age, and citizens of the United States, or in any way abridged, except for participation in rebellion, or other crime, the basis of representation therein shall be reduced in the proportion which the number of such male citizens shall bear to the whole number of male citizens twenty-one years of age in such State.

SECTION 3.   No person shall be a Senator or Representative in Congress, or elector of President and Vice President, or hold any office, civil or military, under the United States, or under any State, who, having previously taken an oath, as a member of Congress, or as an officer of the United States, or as a member of any State legislature, or as an executive or judicial officer of any State, to support the Constitution of the United States, shall have engaged in insurrection or rebellion against the same, or given aid or comfort to the enemies thereof. But Congress may by a vote of two-thirds of each House, remove such disability.

SECTION 4.   The validity of the public debt of the United States, authorized by law, including debts incurred for payment of pensions and bounties for services in suppressing insurrection or rebellion, shall not be questioned. But neither the United States nor any State shall assume or pay any debt or obligation incurred in aid of insurrection or rebellion against the United States, or any claim for the loss or emancipation of any slave; but all such debts, obligations and claims shall be held illegal and void.

SECTION 5.   The Congress shall have power to enforce, by appropriate legislation, the provisions of this article.

Fifteenth Amendment
(Ratified in 1870)

SECTION 1.   The right of citizens of the United States to vote shall not be denied or abridged by the United States or by any State on account of race, color, or previous condition of servitude.

SECTION 2.   The Congress shall have power to enforce this article by appropriate legislation.

Nineteenth Amendment
(Ratified in 1920)

The right of citizens of the United States to vote shall not be denied or abridged by the United States or by any State on account of sex.

Congress shall have power to enforce this article by appropriate legislation.

Twentieth Amendment
(Ratified in 1933)

SECTION 1.   The terms of the President and Vice President shall end at noon on the 20th day of January, and the terms of Senators and Representatives at noon on the 3d day of January, of the years in which such terms would have ended if this article had not been ratified; and the terms of their successors shall then begin.

SECTION 2. The Congress shall assemble at least once in every year, and such meeting shall begin at noon on the 3d day of January, unless they shall by law appoint a different day.

SECTION 3. If, at the time fixed for the beginning of the term of the President, the President elect shall have died, the Vice President elect shall become President. If a President shall not have been chosen before the time fixed for the beginning of his term, or if the President elect shall have failed to qualify, then the Vice President elect shall act as President until a President shall have qualified; and the Congress may by law provide for the case wherein neither a President elect nor a Vice President elect shall have qualified, declaring who shall then act as President, or the manner in which one who is to act shall be selected, and such persons shall act accordingly until a President or Vice President shall have qualified.

SECTION 4. The Congress may by law provide for the case of the death of any of the persons from whom the House of Representatives may choose a President whenever the right of choice shall have devolved upon them, and for the case of the death of any of the persons from whom the Senate may choose a Vice President whenever the right of choice shall have devolved upon them.

SECTION 5. Sections 1 and 2 shall take effect on the 15th day of October following the ratification of this article.

SECTION 6. This article shall be inoperative unless it shall have been ratified as an amendment to the Constitution by the legislatures of three-fourths of the several States within seven years from the date of its submission.

Twenty-second Amendment
(Ratified in 1951)

SECTION 1. No person shall be elected to the office of the President more than twice, and no person who has held the office of President, or acted as President, for more than two years of a term to which some other person was elected President, shall be elected to the office of the President more than once. But this article shall not apply to any person holding the office of President when this Article was proposed by the Congress, and shall not prevent any person who may be holding the office of President, or acting as President, during the term within which this Article becomes operative from holding the office of President or acting as President during the remainder of such term.

SECTION 2. This article shall be inoperative unless it shall have been ratified as an amendment to the Constitution by the legislatures of three-fourths of the several States within seven years from the date of its submission to the States by the Congress.

Twenty-third Amendment
(Ratified in 1961)

SECTION 1. The District constituting the seat of Government of the United States shall appoint in such manner as the Congress may direct:

A number of electors of President and Vice President equal to the whole number of Senators and Representatives in Congress to which the District would be entitled if it were a State, but in no event more than the least populous State; they shall be in addition to those appointed by the States, but they shall be considered, for the purposes of the election of President and Vice President, to be electors appointed by a State; and they shall meet in the District and perform such duties as provided by the twelfth article of amendment.

SECTION 2.   The Congress shall have power to enforce this article by appropriate legislation.

Twenty-fourth Amendment
(Ratified in 1964)

SECTION 1.   The right of citizens of the United States to vote in any primary or other election for President or Vice President, for electors for President or Vice President, or for Senator or Representative in Congress, shall not be denied or abridged by the United States or any State by reason of failure to pay any poll tax or other tax.

SECTION 2.   The Congress shall have power to enforce this article by appropriate legislation.

Twenty-fifth Amendment
(Ratified in 1967)

SECTION 1.   In case of the removal of the President from office or of his death or resignation, the Vice President shall become President.

SECTION 2.   Whenever there is a vacancy in the office of the Vice President, the President shall nominate a Vice President who shall take office upon confirmation by a majority vote of both Houses of Congress.

SECTION 3.   Whenever the President transmits to the President pro tempore of the Senate and the Speaker of the House of Representatives his written declaration that he is unable to discharge the powers and duties of his office, and until he transmits to them a written declaration to the contrary, such powers and duties shall be discharged by the Vice President as Acting President.

SECTION 4.   Whenever the Vice President and a majority of either the principal officers of the executive departments or of such other body as Congress may by law provide, transmit to the President pro tempore of the Senate and the Speaker of the House of Representatives their written declaration that the President is unable to discharge the powers and duties of his office, the Vice President shall immediately assume the powers and duties of the office as Acting President.

Thereafter, when the President transmits to the President pro tempore of the Senate and the Speaker of the House of Representatives his written declaration that no inability exists, he shall resume the powers and duties of his office unless the Vice President and a majority of either the principal officers of the executive department or of such other body as Congress may by law provide, transmit within four days to the President pro tempore of the Senate and the Speaker of the House of Representatives their written declaration that the President is unable to discharge the powers and duties of his office. Thereupon Congress shall decide the issue, assembling within forty-eight hours for that purpose if not in session. If the Congress, within twenty-one days after receipt of the latter written declaration, or, if Congress is not in session, within twenty-one days after Congress is required to assemble, determines by two-thirds vote of both Houses that the President is unable to discharge the powers and duties of his office, the Vice President shall continue to discharge the same as Acting President; otherwise, the President shall resume the powers and duties of his office.

INDEX

Note: Starred words are defined in the Glossary.